Forbidden fruits & Forgotten vegetables

"A Guide to Cooking
with Ethnic, Exotic,
and Neglected Produce"

by George and Nancy Marcus

photography by Will Brown

ST. MARTIN'S PRESS/NEW YORK

To David and Paul
who staunchly tried everything

Library of Congress Cataloging in Publication Data

Marcus, Nancy.
Forbidden fruits and forgotten vegetables.

1. Cookery (Fruit) 2. Cookery (Vegetables)
I. Marcus, George. II. Title.
TX811.M36   641.6'4   81-16553
ISBN 0-312-29826-9   AACR2
ISBN 0-312-29827-7 (pbk.)

For information, write: St. Martin's Press,
175 Fifth Avenue, New York, N.Y. 10010
Manufactured in the United States of America

Design by Manuela Paul
10 9 8 7 6 5 4 3 2 1

First Edition

Contents

Acknowledgments

Many ingredients went into the preparation of this cookbook:

The encouragement of those who, from the beginning, were convinced that it should come to fruition, especially Charlotte Sheedy, Barbara Held, and Sara Bershtel.

The generosity of those who described their traditions and shared their recipes with us, especially Eva Ray and Haim Shapiro.

The helpfulness of those who made everything come together: those who let us pick from their gardens and orchards, those who sent us out-of-season produce just when we needed it, those who helped us search out obscure sources and documentation in libraries, those who tasted and offered suggestions.

Without a blending of these ingredients, this undertaking could not have been accomplished.

Index

Appetizers

Soups

Main Courses

CHICKEN DISHES
Chicken in Pomegranate Sauce   105
Chicken Pie with Salsify and Carrots   122
Chicken with Papaya   78

FISH DISHES
Cod and Swiss Chard Casserole   135
Grilled Mackerel with Fennel   26
Seafood Gumbo   68

MEAT DISHES
Beef with Snow Peas, Broccoli, and Sunchokes   42
Caribbean Stew with Plantains   94
Dutch Kale and Potato Stew (Stampot)   52
Lamb Curry with Mashed Papaya   77
North African Lamb Stew with Okra   69
Stewed Beef with Quinces   112
Turkish Celery Root and Lamb Stew   4

VEGETABLE DISHES
Bengali Stewed Vegetables with Plantains   95
Mango Curry   59
Quimbombo (Cuban Okra Stew)   70

Eggs and Omelettes

Dandelion Frittata   21
Kale and Eggs   52

Pancakes and Fritters

Pasta Dishes

Vegetable Dishes

BAKED/SOUFFLÉED

BOILED/STEWED

Salads

Sauces

Pickles, Relishes, and Chutneys

Desserts

Cakes, Cookies, and Breads

Frosting

Jellies, Marmalades, and Butters

Introduction

Growing up in urban America, we were raised on peas and potatoes, carrots and string beans, with occasional helpings of cauliflower and squash. It would never have occurred to our mothers to serve dandelions or bake with persimmons, to buy papayas or fry plantains, although the former could have been seen downtown in Italian markets and the latter bought uptown in Spanish *bodegas*. Few such specialties crossed town, not to mention the country or the seas, to tempt supermarket shoppers into trying the unique foods of other regions or cultures. Thirty years ago, assimilation had not yet extended as far as the kitchen, and even neighbors in immigrant communities rarely tasted from a culinary melting pot.

Today all that has changed. America has become aware of food. The popularity of "gourmet" cooking, extensive travel, and the availability of a wider range of ingredients have excited cooks into experimenting with new foods and diverse traditions of preparing them. It is not uncommon now to see kale and mangoes vying with corn and tomatoes in produce bins, not just in specialty shops and ethnic groceries but in chain stores as well.

Over the last few years, as these foods became relatively common, we became more and more eager to include them in our cooking. Although most of the foods were familiar to us, we knew few methods for preparing them—and very little about their history and characteristics. When we started to look, we could find no comprehensive source to help satisfy our curiosity, and thus this cookbook evolved. It is the culmination of research, kitchen testing, the fruits of our travels abroad, and the gastronomic recollections of friends from various backgrounds.

Our goal has been to present a well-rounded introduction to the selection, preparation, and use of some of the unusual and exotic fruits and vegetables that we have enjoyed. We have also included a number of fruits and vegetables that are actually abundant here; neglected by most Americans these are generally used within certain groups or locales—collards by Southerners, dandelions by Italians, celery root by those of northern European stock. Two areas of specialty produce are not covered: the distinctive vegetables of French *haute cuisine*—leeks, artichokes, asparagus—and the entire range of peculiarly Oriental foods—winter melon, lotus root, burdock, and the like—as these are dealt with at great length in numerous other cookbooks.

The fruits and vegetables that we have chosen are not necessarily costly. Indeed, when they are in season, many can be quite reasonable, while plantains and greens, for example, are always a good buy. Each chapter in this book identifies when these foods are in season, explains how to select them in the market, and describes how to prepare them for cooking.

This is not a vegetarian cookbook, although it offers many ideas for the expansion of vegetarian menus with tasty and nutritious foods. In compiling this cookbook, it was not necessary to concoct scores of recipes, for traditional methods abound. The recipes are mainly simple ones, using ingredients generally at hand, although some ethnic dishes did require us to stretch this rule. They use standard cooking techniques, and one does not need special talent to cook with unusual fruits and vegetables. The dishes range from soups, stews, and omelettes to purées, pickles, and pies. We have selected them from as wide a range of traditions as possible to provide a well-rounded guide to the authentic uses of these unusual, exotic, and neglected fruits and vegetables.

Celery Root

Celery root, or celeriac, is the paradigm of the undeservedly neglected vegetable. For years, commentators in America have lauded its flavor and lamented its scarcity, as Miss Beecher did in the middle of the last century in her *Domestic Receipt Book*—"This is very good, and but little known." In the previous century, however, celery root had been held in high enough esteem to be recommended by John Randolph, Jr., in his *Treatise on Gardening by a Citizen of Virginia*. Early settlers in Virginia had been required to plant gardens to insure against famine, and winter vegetables such as celery root, which Randolph said grew "as large as turneps," were particularly valuable when other crops were scarce. Even today this root remains important as a winter vegetable, especially in the Scandinavian countries, France, Germany, and eastern Europe.

Although Americans often have their first dish of celery root while they are traveling in Europe, its taste and aroma, reminiscent of celery, are hardly foreign to the palate. Instead of the thick, crispy stalks of celery, this variety has a large, edible swollen knob that forms just below the ground and gives it its alternative names: knob, or turnip-rooted, celery. Its botanical name, *Apium graveolens rapaceum* ("strong-smelling, turniplike parsley"), reveals its relationship to parsley, both vegetables having a common ancestor in the herb smallage, which originated in the Mediterranean region in ancient times. But celery root—and celery—were probably not fully developed until modern times, not much earlier than the fifteenth or sixteenth century.

HOW TO SELECT CELERY ROOT

If there is any doubt as to which gnarled knob in a produce bin is celery root, the pleasant, celerylike aroma will identify it immediately. A winter crop, celery root is most abundant in markets from fall through early spring. The roundish knobs, with their light brown, pocked skin and many small roots, are most likely to range from 2 to 4 inches in diameter, although considerably larger roots do appear. Choose medium-size vegetables that feel solid and heavy and are not soft on top or spongy when pressed; larger roots may be woody or have hollow centers. The roots will keep for many weeks in a cold place or in the refrigerator, but, as with most vegetables, celery root is at its best when eaten soon after it is harvested.

HOW TO PREPARE CELERY ROOT

Celery root is a common ingredient in much European winter cooking, from Scandinavia to the Balkans. Boiled, it is served with basic sauces—butter, cream, cheese, béchamel; puréed, it is combined with potatoes in soups and soufflés. It is diced or sliced for frying and for stews and soups, and it is hollowed out as a shell for stuffing. Celery root is also used raw in salads and is perhaps best known in the French céleri rémoulade (julienne strips of celery root tossed in a mustardy mayonnaise, see recipe on this page). Other salad recipes traditionally call for parboiled celery root, the whole, peeled knobs boiled about 20 minutes and then refreshed in cold water. This is said to remove any bitterness, but with fresh and young vegetables, this step is not actually necessary.

Celery root is customarily peeled before it is cooked; this is best done with a potato peeler or paring knife. The tops and secondary roots should be trimmed, the dirt washed from the surface or crevices, and the scattered root spots dug out as with a potato. To prevent discoloration after peeling and slicing, celery root should be dropped into acidulated water (water with vinegar added, 1 teaspoon to a quart).

Céleri Rémoulade

This crudité is ubiquitous in the charcuteries and restaurants of France.

INGREDIENTS
½ cup mayonnaise

2 teaspoons prepared Dijon mustard
2 teaspoons wine vinegar
¼ teaspoon salt
2 celery roots, peeled and cut into matchstick slices

Garnish
lettuce
2 tablespoons chopped parsley

In a bowl, combine mayonnaise, mustard, vinegar, and salt, and mix until very smooth and well blended. Toss celery roots with dressing and serve on lettuce as an appetizer or salad, garnished with chopped parsley. *Serves 4.*

Winter Vegetable Soup

INGREDIENTS
3 tablespoons butter
1 celery root, peeled and diced
2 carrots, diced
1 turnip, diced
1 medium onion, sliced
6 cups boiling water
½ cup thin spaghetti, broken into small pieces
1 teaspoon salt
½ teaspoon paprika
2 tablespoons chopped parsley

Melt butter in a soup kettle, add celery root, carrots, turnip, and sliced onion, and sauté over a low flame 10 minutes, mixing occasionally. Add 6 cups boiling water and cook over medium flame, covered. After 20 minutes, add broken spaghetti and cook for 25 minutes more. Add salt, paprika, and parsley, and continue to cook 5 minutes longer. *Serves 6.*

Turkish Celery Root and Lamb Stew

INGREDIENTS
2 celery roots, peeled and cut into ¾-inch cubes
3 tablespoons butter
1 pound lean lamb, cut into 1-inch cubes
1 onion, coarsely chopped
1 cup boiling water
½ teaspoon salt
¼ teaspoon pepper
2 eggs, lightly beaten
3 tablespoons lemon juice

Drop cubed celery roots into boiling salted water and cook until they can be just pierced with a fork—about 5 minutes—and drain. Melt butter in a large skillet over moderate flame and brown meat on all sides. Add onion and parboiled celery roots and sauté for 5 minutes, stirring well so that onion and celery roots are well coated. Add 1 cup boiling water, salt, and pepper, cover, and cook over moderate heat about 45 minutes, or until meat is tender.

In a separate saucepan, combine beaten eggs and lemon juice and cook over very low heat, slowly adding the liquid from the stew (which should measure about ¾ cup), stirring constantly until the sauce thickens—about 10 minutes. Do not allow sauce to boil. Arrange meat and celery root on a platter and pour sauce over. Serve immediately. *Serves 4.*

Scandinavian Fish Soup

INGREDIENTS
Stock:
1 2-pound whiting or haddock, cleaned
1 onion, coarsely chopped
1 carrot, diced

1 bay leaf
2 sprigs parsley
1 teaspoon salt
6 whole peppercorns

Soup:
1 celery root, peeled and diced
1 onion, diced
1 carrot, diced
1 potato, diced

Garnish
6 tablespoons sour cream
chopped dill

In a soup kettle, combine the whole fish with onion, carrot, bay leaf, parsley, salt, and peppercorns, and cover with 8 cups of water. Bring to a boil and simmer until fish is tender and can be flaked easily, about 30 minutes. Remove fish and strain liquid through a sieve, pressing on vegetables to extract juices. Return stock to kettle; add diced celery root, onion, carrot, and potato, and bring to a boil. Reduce heat and simmer until the vegetables are tender—about 20 minutes. Meanwhile carefully remove the flesh of the fish from the bones and flake, returning it to soup when vegetables are tender. Ladle into bowls and garnish each with a tablespoon of sour cream and dill.
Serves 6.

Stuffed Celery Root

INGREDIENTS
2 large celery roots, peeled and cut in half
1 onion, finely chopped
1 carrot, shredded
2 tablespoons butter
¼ teaspoon salt
⅛ teaspoon pepper
1 tablespoon grated Parmesan cheese
1 tablespoon melted butter

Drop celery-root halves into a pot of boiling salted water and boil until tender, about 20 to 30 minutes. Remove from pot and refresh under cold water. Form a hollow in each half by scooping out pulp, leaving a shell about ½-inch thick. Chop pulp and sauté with onion and carrot in 2 tablespoons butter. Add salt and pepper and mix well. Add two tablespoons water to skillet, cover, and cook for about 10 minutes, or until the vegetables become softened.

Preheat oven to 375 degrees. Stuff the vegetable mixture into each celery root, mounding as necessary, and place in buttered baking dish. Sprinkle tops with grated cheese and drizzle with melted butter. Bake for about a half-hour, until well heated and tops are brown. Serve as an accompaniment to broiled meat or roasts.
Serves 4.

Mashed Celery Root and Potatoes

INGREDIENTS
2 celery roots, peeled and quartered
½ pound potatoes, quartered
1 tablespoon butter
¼ cup milk
1 teaspoon salt
⅛ teaspoon white pepper

Garnish
2 tablespoons chopped parsley

Cook celery roots in boiling salted water for 10 minutes. Add potatoes and continue cooking for about 20 minutes more, or until celery root and potatoes are tender. Drain vegetables, add butter and milk, and mash with a fork or potato masher until smooth. Season with salt and pepper and garnish with chopped parsley.
Serves 4.

Celery Root Sauté

INGREDIENTS
2 celery roots, peeled and sliced into ¼-inch-thick rounds
4 tablespoons olive oil
2 tablespoons lemon juice
¼ teaspoon salt
⅛ teaspoon white pepper

Garnish
1 tablespoon finely chopped parsley

In a large frying pan, sauté celery roots in olive oil over medium flame until the edges begin to brown. Add lemon juice, salt, pepper, and ¼ cup water. Cover and cook over low heat about 20 minutes, or until celery root is soft. Sprinkle with chopped parsley and serve.
Serves 4.

German Marinated Celery Root Salad

INGREDIENTS
2 celery roots, peeled
2 scallions, or 1 small onion, finely sliced
2 tablespoons salad oil
¼ cup wine vinegar
½ teaspoon salt
white pepper (to taste)
½ teaspoon sugar

Drop whole celery roots into boiling salted water and boil until they can easily be pierced with a fork—about 20 to 30 minutes. Remove from pot and allow to cool. Cut roots in half and then into ⅛-inch slices. Place in a salad bowl and sprinkle with sliced scallion or onion. To prepare dressing, combine oil, vinegar, salt, pepper, sugar, and 2 tablespoons water and mix well. Pour over celery root slices, toss, and allow to marinate in refrigerator for 1 hour before serving.
Serves 4.

Chayote

To those whose shopping is restricted to supermarkets, the chayote will most likely be unknown. But to those who venture into Oriental groceries or marvel at the odd, exotic produce heaped outside Spanish *bodegas*—or, to those who have enjoyed the cuisine of New Orleans, where these pale green, furrowed vegetables are a local specialty—the chayote may be quite familiar. A native of Central America, this member of the squash and cucumber family (*Sechium edule*) was being grown by the Indians when Cortes first set foot in Mexico, and it has since traveled widely, which explains its appearance in markets serving diverse ethnic populations. It is a staple of much of Latin America and is known also in the southern United States, North Africa, and France, and grows as far afield as Indonesia and Australia.

Chayotes were first described for Europeans by the Spaniard Francisco Hernandez, whose mid-sixteenth century Latin texts tell of the curiosities he encountered during his travels in New Spain. Using the Aztec name *chayotli* and describing the fruit as "like a hedgehog"—a reference to the soft spines that appear on its skin—he noted its widespread use: "The fruit is eaten cooked and is sold in the markets everywhere."

The name *chayote*, close to its antecedent in the Aztec tongue, is used in most Spanish-speaking countries in the Americas. Brazilians and some West Indians call it *chuchu* or *chocho* (which became *choko* in Australia and Southeast Asia), although another name, *christophine*, has also been adopted in the Caribbean. The Chinese name likens its deeply grooved surface and its pear shape to the hands of Buddha held together in prayer. A similar image is alluded to in the name *mirliton*, by which chayotes are known in Louisiana: While *mirliton* is usually translated from French as "reed pipe," it can refer more specifically to those "reed pipes" made by blowing on a blade of grass held tightly between clasped hands.

[9]

HOW TO SELECT CHAYOTES

Chayotes can be found throughout the year in Oriental and Spanish-American markets, although not necessarily at the same time, the supplies apparently being derived from different sources. Locally grown chayotes are most abundant after their relatively long growing season, in the fall and early winter. There are several types, ranging in shape from nearly smooth and oblong to deeply ridged and pear shaped; they vary in length from 5 to 8 inches and in weight from ½ to 1 pound, while their color will go from a true pastel green to an off-white. Chayotes are firm and crisp when ready for use; avoid vegetables that are soft and wrinkled or have blemishes. Firm chayotes will keep as long as a month in the refrigerator.

HOW TO PREPARE CHAYOTES

Any squash recipe can be easily adapted for chayotes, although they are generally blander in taste and firmer in substance than most soft-skinned squashes and can be cooked longer without falling apart. They are not eaten raw but are cooked both as a vegetable and as a sweet. Most characteristically, in Latin American and creole cooking they are stuffed with combinations of meat, cheese, or shrimp (traditional in New Orleans). They can be boiled and served very simply with butter or other standard sauces, or cold in salads; they can also be deep fried, baked, mashed, or included among the starchy roots and squashes in the large stews typically prepared throughout Latin America. As a sweet, the boiled flesh is combined with fruits and nuts and stuffed back in the shells, or they are made into puddings, baked in pies and tarts, or made into sauces, jellies, or jams.

For stuffing, chayotes are usually cut in half and boiled until tender, about 30 minutes. The single seed and the fibrous core that encases it are removed and the flesh is cut out so that a shell about ¼-inch thick remains. For most other recipes, chayotes are peeled first, which is best done with a vegetable parer, releasing an aroma of fresh cut grass. They may then be cut into slices or cubes and boiled, steamed, or sautéed; spices added during boiling enhance their subtle flavor.

Puerto Rican Chayote and Eggs

INGREDIENTS
¼ pound diced cooked ham
1 green pepper, chopped
1 onion, chopped
1 tomato, chopped
1 clove garlic, minced
2 tablespoons olive oil
2 chayotes, peeled and cut into ½-inch cubes
½ teaspoon salt
4 eggs, well beaten

In a large skillet, sauté ham, green pepper, onion, tomato, and garlic in oil over medium heat until vegetables are soft, about 10 minutes, mixing occasionally. Add cubed chayotes, salt, and ½ cup water, and continue to cook until chayote becomes translucent and tender—about 20 to 30 minutes—and the water has just about all evaporated. Add beaten eggs and cook slowly, stirring, until eggs are set.
Serves 4.

Indonesian Boiled Choko

INGREDIENTS
2 chayotes, peeled and cut into 1-inch cubes
1 onion, coarsely chopped
1 fresh whole chili pepper
½ teaspoon salt

Place cubed chayotes in a saucepan with chopped onion, whole chili pepper, and salt, and cover with water. Bring to a boil and cook covered until chayote is tender and easily pierced with a fork, about 15 minutes. Drain in colander, remove chili pepper, and serve hot.
Serves 4.

New Orleans Stuffed Mirliton

INGREDIENTS
2 chayotes, cut in half
1 medium onion, finely chopped
1 clove garlic, minced
2 tablespoons butter
½ pound shrimp, boiled, peeled, deveined, and diced
2 tablespoons chopped parsley
cayenne (to taste)
¼ teaspoon salt
¼ cup bread crumbs
2 tablespoons melted butter

Boil chayote halves in water for about 30 minutes, until they are tender and can be pierced easily with a fork. Drain and allow to cool. Remove seed and core, scoop out pulp and reserve, leaving a shell about ¼-inch thick all around. In a frying pan, sauté onion and garlic in 2 tablespoons butter until translucent. Mash pulp of chayote and add to pan with shrimp, parsley, a dash of cayenne (or more to taste), and salt, and continue to sauté 5 minutes longer, stirring occasionally.

Preheat oven to 350 degrees. Fill shells with pulp-and-shrimp mixture, mounding it as necessary. Sprinkle tops with bread crumbs, drizzle with melted butter, and place in baking dish with ½ cup water. Bake for about 30 minutes, until chayotes are heated through and tops are well browned.
Serves 4.

Chayote Stuffed with Cheese

INGREDIENTS
2 chayotes, cut in half
2 tablespoons butter
1 medium onion, finely chopped
½ cup grated Edam, Swiss, or cheddar cheese
½ teaspoon salt
¼ teaspoon pepper

¼ cup bread crumbs
2 tablespoons melted butter

Boil chayote halves in water until they are tender and can easily be pierced with a fork, about 30 minutes. Drain and allow to cool so they may be handled. Remove seed and core and scoop out pulp, leaving a shell about ¼-inch thick. In a frying pan, melt butter and sauté onion until softened and translucent. Mash chayote pulp and add to pan, continuing to sauté for several minutes more. In a bowl, combine sautéed mixture with grated cheese, season with salt and pepper, and mix well. Preheat oven to 350 degrees. Fill shells with mixture, mounding it as necessary. Sprinkle tops with bread crumbs, drizzle with melted butter, and place in baking dish with ½ cup water. Bake for about 30 minutes, until chayotes are well heated and tops are brown.
Serves 4.

Caribbean Chocho Sauce

INGREDIENTS
2 chayotes, peeled and cubed
6 cloves
¼ cup sugar
juice of 1 lemon or lime

Boil cubed chayotes in water to which cloves have been added for about 20 minutes, until chayote is very tender. Drain and remove cloves. Mash chayote well, add sugar and lemon or lime juice, and serve like applesauce.
Serves 4.

Chayote à la Creole

INGREDIENTS
2 chayotes, peeled and cut lengthwise into eighths
1 onion, chopped
1 clove garlic, minced
3 tablespoons olive oil
1 sixteen-ounce can tomatoes, drained well and chopped
1 tablespoon chopped parsley
⅛ teaspoon dried thyme
¼ teaspoon salt
pinch cayenne

Garnish
2 tablespoons chopped parsley

Boil chayote sections in water for about 15 minutes, until just tender. Sauté onion and garlic in oil in a large frying pan until onion is translucent. Add boiled chayotes, chopped tomatoes, parsley, thyme, salt, and cayenne and mix well. Cover and simmer over low heat for a half-hour. Remove lid and continue to cook until sauce is thick and chayotes are quite tender, about 15 minutes longer. Garnish with chopped parsley and serve with boiled rice.
Serves 4.

Dandelion

From time immemorial, as winter passed and the first shoots pushed up from the earth, country folk took to the woods and fields to gather the delicate spring greens, local custom distinguishing those that were fit for the table from those that were inedible. After the long winter, during which few or no fresh vegetables had been eaten, these greens were considered to have a cleansing and renewing effect upon the body. The medicinal properties of the dandelion were especially prized in the medieval pharmacy, and its respected position was signaled by its botanical name, *Taraxacum officinale*, or "healing bitter herb." The diuretic effect of its bitter leaves is reflected in one of the names by which dandelion used to be popularly known in England, piss-a-bed, and by which, as *pissenlit*, it is still widely called in France today.

The dandelion—the ragged leaves of which remind the French of a lion's teeth, or *dents-de-lion*—is not native to America but is a plant that grew wild in Europe and Asia. It was served in salads and stewed as a potherb by the Romans, and some think that this was the original bitter herb prescribed in the Bible for the Passover meal. Early settlers brought the dandelion to these shores, but for the colonial pharmacopoeia rather than for food. Its familiar windblown seed puffs, carried from cultivated herb gardens to the newly ploughed fields, soon established it here as a very common wildflower—or weed. Although they are detested by gardeners, dandelions are grown commercially for food and are touted for their nutritive value and for the tangy flavor they give to traditional dishes cooked by Italian-Americans, Southerners, and the Pennsylvania Dutch.

HOW TO SELECT DANDELIONS

April and May are the height of the dandelion season; after that, they tend to become tough and quite bitter, although a second crop of young plants sometimes appears in markets in late summer and fall. Buy them when they look fresh and are crisp, avoiding plants that have yellowed leaves. Cultivated varieties are most likely to be found in health-food stores and Italian markets; they have longer leaves and are a little lighter in color and less bitter than wild plants. Wild dandelions, however, are just as suitable for the table if they are picked young—before flowers form—and precautions are taken to assure that the plants have not been sprayed with weed killers. Dandelions will keep for several days in a crisper or a plastic bag in the refrigerator.

HOW TO PREPARE DANDELIONS

Dandelions are usually quite dirty and should be washed thoroughly and picked over well, with the roots, buds, and any flowers removed. They may be cooked like spinach and are especially good creamed or puréed; they are also frequently among the Greens (Chapter 5) boiled as potherbs in the South. However, dandelions are most delicious when used in salads alone or combined with other greens, the bitter lion's-tooth leaves giving a bracing digestive fillip to a rich meal. They may be served with a simple French dressing but often, in European and American traditions, dandelion salads are eaten with a hot dressing of bacon fat or oil, which gently wilts the greens as it is poured over them. One pound of leaves is sufficient for a salad of four.

Dandelion and Swiss Chard Soup

Any combination of leafy greens can be used to prepare this simple Italian peasant soup.

INGREDIENTS
1 pound dandelion leaves, well washed and torn in half
1 pound Swiss Chard (see Chapter 16), leaves only,
    washed well and coarsely shredded
½ teaspoon salt
4 cups boiling water
4 ¾-inch-thick slices stale Italian bread, well toasted

1 clove garlic, sliced
1 tablespoon fine olive oil

Garnish
Grated Parmesan cheese

Put greens in a deep kettle with only the water that clings to them after washing, add salt, cover tightly, and cook over moderate heat until reduced, about 15 minutes. Add 4 cups boiling water, cover, and cook slowly until greens are very tender, about a half-hour. Meanwhile, rub toasted bread on both sides with cut garlic and place a piece of toast in each of the soup bowls. When greens are tender, add olive oil, stir, and ladle soup into bowls over bread. Serve with Parmesan cheese.
Serves 4.

Pennsylvania Dutch Wilted Dandelion Salad

INGREDIENTS
1 pound dandelion leaves, washed, drained well,
     and torn into 2-inch lengths
1 teaspoon butter
¾ cup sour cream
1 egg, well beaten
2 teaspoons sugar
1 tablespoon vinegar
½ teaspoon salt
¼ teaspoon pepper

Arrange dandelion leaves in a salad bowl. Melt butter in a saucepan. Combine sour cream, egg, sugar, vinegar, salt, and pepper in a bowl and mix well. Add to saucepan and stir until the dressing begins to thicken and come to a boil. Pour over the dandelion greens immediately, toss well, and serve.
Serves 4.

Wilted Dandelion Salad with Bacon

INGREDIENTS
1 pound dandelion leaves, washed, drained well,
  and torn into 2-inch lengths
4 slices bacon, cut into 1-inch pieces
3 tablespoons vinegar
½ teaspoon salt
freshly ground pepper (to taste)
pinch sugar

Arrange dandelion leaves in a salad bowl. In a frying pan, fry bacon over medium heat until crisp. Remove, drain on paper toweling, and distribute on dandelion leaves. Add vinegar, salt, pepper, and sugar to the bacon fat in the pan and bring to a boil. Immediately pour over salad, toss well, and serve.
Serves 4.

Wilted Dandelion Salad with Croutons

INGREDIENTS
1 pound dandelion leaves, washed, drained well,
  and torn into 2-inch lengths
½ teaspoon salt
freshly ground pepper (to taste)
½ cup olive oil
2 thick slices stale white bread, cut into ½-inch cubes
juice of half lemon

Arrange dandelion leaves in a salad bowl and season with salt and pepper. In a frying pan, heat olive oil over medium flame, add cubed white bread, and fry until bread becomes brown on all sides. Pour immediately over the dandelion greens and toss well. Sprinkle with lemon juice and serve.
Serves 4.

Dandelion Frittata

Serve this Italian omelette cut in wedges.

INGREDIENTS
½ pound dandelion leaves, washed, drained well, and torn in half
1 tablespoon olive oil
1 tablespoon butter
4 eggs
1 tablespoon milk
2 tablespoons grated Parmesan cheese
¼ teaspoon salt
freshly ground pepper (to taste)

Heat oil and butter together over medium heat in a 9-inch oven-proof frying pan. Add dandelion leaves, reduce heat, and cook covered for about 10 minutes, or until leaves are tender, stirring once to make sure that top leaves are also cooked. Meanwhile, in a bowl, combine eggs, milk, grated cheese, salt, and pepper, and beat until frothy. Pour over tender dandelion leaves in frying pan and cook slowly until top has begun to set and bottom is brown. Pass under broiler and cook until top is well set and lightly brown.
Serves 2.

Dandelion Salad with Anchovy Dressing

INGREDIENTS
1 pound dandelion leaves, washed, drained well,
   and torn into 2-inch lengths
1 tablespoon anchovy paste
3 tablespoons olive oil
juice of half lemon

Arrange dandelion leaves in a salad bowl. In a separate bowl, combine anchovy paste with oil and lemon juice and mix until ingredients are well combined. Pour over dandelion leaves and toss.
Serves 4.

$\mathcal{F}$ennel

Fennel is used "especially in Southern Italy," the author of *The Three Musketeers* instructs us in his dictionary of cooking. "It is eaten like celery," continues Dumas, and evoking a picture of simple country life, he adds: "It is not uncommon to come upon peasants carrying their bunch of fennel under the arm and, with some bread, making their lunch or dinner of it." The cool and crisp licorice-tasting bulb of the fennel (*Foeniculum vulgare dulce*), known in Italy as *finocchio*, must have quenched their thirst and satisfied.

For a long time fennel was—and to a great extent still is—restricted to the tables of Italy and France. But even two centuries ago, Diderot's *Encyclopedia* noted the superiority of the Italian variety to any the French could grow, praising the "flavor, delicacy, and aroma" of the fennel cultivated there.

In America, too, fennel is most popular among those of Italian heritage. However, a century and half ago, it had been recommended to Thomas Jefferson for cultivation in his garden at Monticello by Thomas Appleton, his correspondent in Italy, who over the years supplied him with "trees, cuttings, plants, and seeds" as well as his Italian wines. In 1824, Appleton sent him fennel seeds with this acclamatory description: "The Fennel, is beyond, every other vegetable, Delicious. It greatly resembles in appearance the largest size Sellery, perfectly white, and there is no vegetable, equals it in flavour. It is eaten at Dessert, crude, and, with, or without Dry Salt, indeed, I preferred it to every other vegetable, or to any fruit." With such a glowing review, one wonders why it never gathered a wider following in America.

HOW TO SELECT FENNEL

Fennel, in season from October through April, is certain to appear in Italian markets, but it is now commonly sold in some supermarkets as well. Often it is mislabeled *anise*, an herb whose licorice-flavor seeds are used as a seasoning. Some produce dealers display fennel sitting in a pail of water with its long stalks of feathery green leaves intact; more often, the stalks are trimmed to about 8 inches in length, so that only a few small leaves remain. Fennel bulbs should be crisp and white to light green in color; avoid those that are turning brown. The outermost part of the bulb may be tough and rubbery, but if the stalks appear firm and fresh, the inside should be succulent. Fennel should be stored like celery; it will stay in a crisper or plastic bag in the refrigerator for several weeks.

HOW TO PREPARE FENNEL

While all parts of fennel are edible, the bulb is savored as a vegetable. Its true flavor and refreshing crispness come through best when it is eaten raw, as an appetizer, a salad, or a dessert. In Italy, it is eaten as all three, in pinzimonio ("with the fingers"), dipped in the sauce with this name: fine olive oil seasoned with salt and pepper. The licorice taste associated with fennel mellows somewhat with cooking and adds a subtle flavor to soups, sauces, and soufflés. Fennel may be boiled, fried, and sautéed, and it often accompanies fish dishes and goes especially well with tomatoes.

Fennel is very clean; if the outer branches are tough or discolored, they should be removed, but the inner branches need not even be washed. The stalks should be trimmed off at the level of the bulb and the bottom edge pared like celery. The bulb should be cut vertically, in half or wedges for serving, or it can be sliced horizontally in rounds, which will separate during cooking much like an onion.

Fennel with Bagna Cauda

Fennel, sweet red pepper, celery, cabbage, and especially cardoons (a vegetable not merely neglected but almost totally unknown in this country) are typically dipped into the hot anchovy-garlic bagna cauda ("hot bath") sauce of the Piedmont region of northern Italy and eaten as an appetizer.

INGREDIENTS
3 tablespoons butter

½ cup olive oil
1 two-ounce can flat fillets of anchovy
3 cloves garlic, very finely sliced
2 fennel bulbs, trimmed and cut lengthwise into eighths

Combine butter and olive oil in a saucepan and add the olive oil from the can of anchovies. Add the garlic and cook over low heat until the garlic has softened and virtually dissolved—about 10 to 15 minutes—taking care that the garlic does not brown. Mince the anchovies very fine and add to the saucepan. Continue to cook slowly, stirring until anchovies disintegrate and the sauce is smooth. Serve sauce hot (keeping it warm over a candle warmer) with fennel—and any other fresh vegetables desired—and crusty Italian bread.
Makes about 1 cup sauce.

Fennel à la Grecque

INGREDIENTS
¼ cup olive oil
¼ cup lemon juice
½ teaspoon salt
2 tablespoons minced onion
⅛ teaspoon dried thyme
1 small celery stalk sliced with leaves
3 sprigs parsley
1 sprig fennel leaves
10 peppercorns
10 whole coriander seeds
3 fennel bulbs, trimmed and cut lengthwise into quarters

In a saucepan, combine olive oil, lemon juice, salt, onion, and dried thyme with 1½ cups water. Tie together in cheesecloth the celery stalk, parsley, sprig of fennel, peppercorns, and coriander seeds, and add to saucepan. Bring to a boil, cover, and simmer for about 10 minutes. Add fennel bulbs and simmer covered for 40 minutes. Discard cheesecloth and remove fennel from liquid with a slotted spoon. Bring liquid back to a boil and cook until it is reduced to about ½ cup. Pour over fennel, chill, and serve as an appetizer.
Serves 4.

Cream of Fennel Soup

INGREDIENTS
1 fennel bulb, trimmed and sliced crosswise
4 tablespoons butter
2 tablespoons flour
4 cups clear chicken broth
salt (to taste)
2 egg yolks
¼ cup heavy cream

Garnish
1 teaspoon chopped fennel leaves

Stew fennel slices in 2 tablespoons butter in a covered saucepan over medium heat for 10 minutes. In a large enamel saucepan, melt remaining 2 tablespoons butter and add flour, stirring constantly over low heat until well blended. Add broth slowly, continuing to stir until all ingredients are well mixed. Bring to a boil, add fennel, and simmer gently, covered, until fennel is very soft—about 15 minutes. Pour soup through a sieve and rub the fennel through with the back of a wooden spoon, discarding any pulp that remains. Return soup to saucepan and reheat, adding salt to taste if necessary. Beat egg yolks with cream in a bowl and add to soup, stirring constantly. Heat slowly to thicken soup, but do not allow to boil. Garnish with chopped fennel leaves and serve. *Serves 4.*

Grilled Mackerel with Fennel

According to Mrs. Beeton's Book of Household Management *(1861), the use of fennel in English cookery was restricted to a fennel-butter sauce for mackerel.*

INGREDIENTS
4 mackerel (about ¾ pound each), cleaned, heads removed

½ teaspoon salt
freshly ground pepper (to taste)
4 tablespoons coarsely chopped fennel bulb
8 sprigs fennel leaves
1 tablespoon vegetable oil

Garnish
lemon wedges

Wash mackerels and pat dry. Sprinkle each cavity with ⅛ teaspoon salt
and a turn of freshly ground pepper to taste. Fill with 1 tablespoon
chopped fennel and two fennel sprigs. Brush skin of fish with oil and
place on a broiling rack. Grill until fish is done, about 5 minutes on each
side. Garnish with lemon wedges and serve with fennel sauce (See
following recipe).
Serves 4.

Fennel Sauce for Fish

INGREDIENTS
1 small fennel bulb, trimmed
¼ pound butter
4 teaspoons flour
¼ teaspoon salt
1 teaspoon chopped fennel leaves

Drop fennel bulb into salted boiling water and parboil for 3 minutes.
Remove, drain very well, and mince very fine. Melt butter in a saucepan
over low heat and add flour, stirring until smooth. Add ½ cup water and
salt, and continue stirring until sauce is almost to the boiling point and
has become thickened. Add ½ cup finely minced fennel bulb and
simmer several minutes longer. Stir in chopped fennel leaves and serve
with grilled mackerel or with other grilled or poached fish.

Makes approximately 1½ cups.

Macaroni with Fennel

INGREDIENTS
3 fennel bulbs, trimmed and cut crosswise into ½-inch slices
6 tablespoons olive oil
1 pound ziti or other macaroni
½ teaspoon salt
¾ cup grated Parmesan or Romano cheese

Cook fennel in a large pot of salted boiling water until pieces can be just pierced, about 10 minutes. Remove fennel with slotted spoon, reserving boiling water for cooking the macaroni. In a skillet, sauté fennel in oil over moderate heat until it just begins to brown. Remove fennel and set aside. Meanwhile, cook macaroni in the salted boiling water until just soft. Drain macaroni but do not rinse, and put in a large bowl. Pour in hot oil from skillet and mix until macaroni is thoroughly coated. Add salt and ½ cup of the grated cheese, and mix well, letting cheese soften in the hot macaroni. Grease a 9 × 13–inch baking dish and fill with macaroni and cheese mixture. Arrange sautéed fennel on top, sprinkle with remaining ¼ cup grated cheese, and pass under broiler, cooking casserole until cheese has melted and top begins to brown.
Serves 6.

Fried Fennel with Tomato Sauce

INGREDIENTS
1 tablespoon olive oil
1 tablespoon tomato paste
¼ teaspoon salt
4 fennel bulbs, trimmed and cut lengthwise into ½-inch-thick slices
¾ cup flour
oil for frying

Make a simple tomato sauce by combining olive oil, tomato paste, and salt with ¼ cup water in a saucepan, and simmer gently, stirring occasionally, for 20 minutes. Meanwhile, drop slices of fennel into salted, boiling water and boil for 3 minutes. Remove fennel slices, refresh under cold running water, and dry well. Dredge fennel slices in flour and fry in heated oil in a large, heavy frying pan until brown on both sides, about 20 minutes, turning pieces carefully. When fennel is well colored, arrange slices on serving platter and spoon tomato sauce over each slice.
Serves 4.

Fennel Parmesan

INGREDIENTS
1 clove garlic
3 tablespoons olive oil
4 fennel bulbs, trimmed and cut lengthwise into quarters
¼ teaspoon salt
¼ cup grated Parmesan cheese

In a large frying pan, gently fry garlic over low heat in oil until it begins to turn golden. Remove garlic and discard. Add quartered fennel and sauté gently for about 10 minutes, turning carefully to color each side. Sprinkle with salt, add 2 tablespoons water, cover, and cook slowly 15 minutes, or until fennel is tender and the liquid has evaporated. Transfer to serving dish, sprinkle with grated cheese, and serve.
Serves 4.

COLLARDS

MUSTARD

RAPE

TURNIP

Greens
(Collards, Mustard, Rape, Turnip)

While Kale (Chapter 7) and Swiss Chard (Chapter 16) have their own very distinct culinary traditions abroad, leafy greens are often confounded in America, especially in the South, where they are eaten in great abundance. Cabbagey collards, tangy turnip tops, sharp mustard—along with chard, kale, and wild greens such as Dandelions (Chapter 3)—are commonly identified there simply as greens. Used as potherbs, they are combined indiscriminately depending on the season and stewed together as a "mess o' greens," their individuality as blurred in the soul-food pot as it often is in the market or recipe book. Cabbages (*Brassicas*) all, these greens are related to the earliest forms of cabbage eaten in Europe thousands of years ago; there, too, over the ages, they have been cooked interchangeably with a host of other greens as pottage: vegetable soups or stews. European settlers brought the seeds of leafy greens with them for their kitchen gardens in colonial America, and they must have come also with the slave trade, for collards and a type of mustard green are much eaten in Africa today. The curly mustard greens are also common farther east, adding their pungency to the dishes of India, China, and Japan. Rape (or broccoletti di rape), a cabbage green now appearing more widely in markets, is closely allied with turnip tops; it is eaten throughout Italy and was until recently restricted here almost entirely to the tables of Italo-Americans.

[31]

HOW TO SELECT GREENS

Collards and mustard greens are available the year round, although they appear to be freshest and most vibrant in color in the early spring. Turnip tops and rape are more likely to appear in the spring and summer. Greens are often lumped together in the produce case, and it takes some experience to distinguish one from the other. Collards have dull-green, cabbagelike leaves on stalks; mustard greens have curly leaves of a pure greenish yellow color, closer in appearance to a lettuce than a cabbage; and the similar-looking rape and turnip tops have central stalks with leaves resembling those on a bunch of broccoli, and often buds and little flowers. Greens are usually sold gathered in bunches weighing from 1 to 3 pounds. Choose those that look fresh and are crispy, avoiding bunches with yellowed leaves. Greens wilt readily and should be stored in a crisper or sealed plastic bag in the refrigerator, where they will stay fresh for several days.

HOW TO PREPARE GREENS

Greens are not generally eaten raw, although the youngest and most tender leaves could be included in salads. Usually greens are boiled first in salted water or steamed with only the water that clings to the leaves after washing. Then they may be treated like spinach, sautéed, stewed, creamed, buttered, or puréed. Southern tradition requires long cooking times for greens—boiling for several hours—but even the toughest greens should achieve sufficient tenderness after being boiled for 20 to 30 minutes.

Greens should be washed well and any yellowed leaves or decayed spots removed before cooking. The stems and central ribs of collards and mustard should be cut away before the leaves are boiled, shredded, or chopped. The thick, woody stalks and tough lower leaves of rape and turnip tops should be discarded, but their thinner stems and their leaves, as well as the florets, can all be eaten. Frozen greens are readily available and may be used in the following recipes for stewed greens.

Mess o' Greens with Corn Dumplings

INGREDIENTS
1 meaty ham bone
3 pounds greens, well washed, stalks removed, and coarsely shredded
1 teaspoon salt
1 teaspoon sugar

Dumplings
¾ cup stone-ground cornmeal
¼ cup flour
1½ teaspoons baking powder
¼ teaspoon salt
1 egg, lightly beaten
⅓ cup milk
1 tablespoon bacon drippings

Garnish
Louisiana-style hot sauce

In a large kettle or soup pot, simmer the ham bone in 6 cups of water, covered, for about an hour. Add shredded greens, salt, and sugar, and simmer covered until greens are very tender, about another hour. Remove bone from pot and allow to cool. Remove meat from bone and cut it into ½-inch cubes. Return meat to pot and reheat.

Meanwhile, prepare dumplings: Sift together cornmeal, flour, baking powder, and salt. Combine beaten egg and milk and add to dry ingredients, mixing with fork until smooth. Stir in bacon drippings and drop by the spoonful onto the greens and cooking liquid. Cover and simmer 15 minutes. Heap greens and ham on a serving dish and arrange dumplings around them. Pour 1 cup of liquid over greens and sprinkle individually to taste with prepared hot sauce.
Serves 6

Stewed Greens with Bacon

Fresh cornbread is traditionally served in the South with stewed greens and dipped into the reserved cooking liquid, called "pot likker."

INGREDIENTS
2 pounds greens, well washed, stalks removed, and coarsely shredded
3 strips bacon, cut into 1-inch pieces
1 onion, sliced
¼ teaspoon salt

Garnish
vinegar
pepper

Fry bacon in a deep kettle over medium heat until crisp. Remove, drain on paper towels, and set aside. Fry onion in the bacon fat until golden. Add greens, salt, and 1 cup water. Cover and cook over medium flame about 20 to 30 minutes, or until greens are tender. Drain, reserving liquid, and transfer to a serving dish, arranging pieces of fried bacon on top. Sprinkle with vinegar and season with a turn of freshly ground pepper to taste. Serve with cornbread and "pot likker."
Serves 4.

Spicy Indian Mustard Greens

INGREDIENTS
4 tablespoons vegetable oil
2 teaspoons black mustard seeds *
1 dried red chili pepper, broken into several pieces
2 pounds mustard greens, well washed, shaken dry, and coarsely shredded
¼ teaspoon salt

* Available in Oriental groceries.

Heat oil over medium flame in a large, deep kettle and add mustard seeds. Seeds will pop off bottom of pot. Continue to heat oil until mustard seeds finish popping. Then drop chili pepper into the oil and carefully add mustard greens, which will cause the oil to splatter if the water has not been shaken off the greens well. Add salt and cook for five minutes, mixing, until greens are well coated with oil and the mustard seeds are dispersed throughout. Cover and cook until greens are tender, about 10 minutes longer. Remove cover, and if any liquid remains in pot, continue to cook until it is evaporated, mixing occasionally. *Serves 4.*

Sautéed Rape with Garlic and Oil

INGREDIENTS
2 pounds rape, washed well, tough parts of stems and leaves removed
4 tablespoons olive oil
1 clove garlic
¼ teaspoon salt
¼ teaspoon freshly ground pepper

Drop rape into a quart of boiling salted water and cook covered until tender, about 15 minutes. Drain in colander, pressing gently with a spoon to squeeze out any remaining water. Heat oil in a skillet over low flame and cook garlic until it becomes soft and just begins to color. Remove garlic and discard. Add rape to oil and season with salt and pepper. Allow to cook very slowly, mixing occasionally, until rape is well flavored, about 10 minutes.
Serves 4.

Sautéed Greens with Vegetables

INGREDIENTS
2 tablespoons butter
2 carrots, finely sliced into rounds
1 onion, sliced
2 green peppers, finely sliced
1½ pound greens, well washed, stalks removed, and coarsely shredded
½ teaspoon salt

Melt butter in large frying pan and sauté carrots, onion, and green peppers over medium heat until well coated. Add 2 tablespoons water, cover tightly, and cook over medium heat for 10 minutes, or until carrots are softened. Add shredded greens and salt, cover, and steam about 20 minutes, or until greens are tender. Stir well before serving. *Serves 4.*

Chinese Pork and Mustard Greens Soup

INGREDIENTS
4 cups chicken broth
¼ pound lean pork, sliced into julienne strips
2 scallions, sliced
½ teaspoon fresh ginger, finely chopped
½ pound mustard greens, well washed and cut into 2-inch lengths
1 tablespoon soy sauce

Bring broth to a boil in a deep soup kettle, add pork, scallions, and ginger, and simmer 5 minutes. Add mustard greens and cook 10 minutes, covered, until greens are reduced. Stir in soy sauce and serve. *Serves 4.*

Jerusalem Artichoke

Of all the vegetables American Indians gave to Europe (potatoes, corn, squash, and tomatoes among them), none was so rapidly adopted by Continental cooks as the Jerusalem artichoke—nor did any fall so quickly out of favor. Domesticated by the Indians, the plants were being cultivated when Samuel de Champlain explored Cape Cod and the St. Lawrence in 1604. These knobby brown tubers soon enriched the diet of New World settlers, and they were among the culinary oddities the explorers brought back to their European homelands, where they almost immediately became a much-coveted delicacy. By 1629, however, the apothecary to King James I, John Parkinson, complained in his *Paradisus in Sole* that they "are by reason of their great increasing, growne to be so common here with us at London, that even the most vulgar begin to despise them, whereas when they were first received among us, they were dainties for a Queene." Ultimately, overabundance turned this at-first-fashionable food into fodder for livestock, which remained its primary use in Europe until it was reintroduced into *haute cuisine* in the nineteenth century.

The tuber of a species of sunflower (*Helianthus tuberosus*) that grows wild in the East from Nova Scotia to Georgia and Alabama, this vegetable was almost immediately associated by Europeans with the artichoke, whose flavor it mildly resembles but to which it is not at all related botanically. Champlain himself reported that the Indians ate "roots which they cultivate . . . having the taste of an artichoke." The connection with Jerusalem, on the other hand, is not so clear, but it seems to have arisen through a corruption of the Italian name given to the sunflower, *girasole*, describing the plant's habit of "turning toward the sun." The French, more appropriately, connected the tubers with native Americans, dubbing them *topinambours*, the name of an Indian tribe from Brazil whose members had apparently visited the French court about the time Jerusalem artichokes were introduced there.

HOW TO SELECT JERUSALEM ARTICHOKES

Jerusalem artichokes are ready for the table after the first frost and are most plentiful in markets throughout the winter and into the spring. The light brown tubers available in America range from about 2 to 5 or 6 inches in length and vary from regular, rounded shapes with fairly smooth skins to large masses with many protuberances and cracks and crevices. (At first glance, the more attenuated varieties might be confused with fresh ginger root.) For ease of cleaning and preparation, select the most regular and smoothest tubers available, making sure that each is firm and crisp; shriveled or soft tubers should be avoided. Jerusalem artichokes are sold loose in produce bins, like potatoes, often with some soil clinging to them. They are now also appearing in markets already cleaned and packaged in cellophane; generally these contain tubers of more regular shape and of uniform size. Jerusalem artichokes should be stored in a cool, dark place or kept in a crisper in the refrigerator, where they will retain their crispness for several weeks. If they are grown at home, the plants should be mulched well and left in the ground to be dug all winter as needed, for they keep best this way.

HOW TO PREPARE JERUSALEM ARTICHOKES

Crisp, fresh Jerusalem artichoke tubers may be enjoyed raw—grated or sliced—in salads or they may be prepared like potatoes: baked, boiled, pan roasted, mashed, sautéed, or fried. The American Indians baked theirs in hot ashes and also added them to soups and stews, while the colonists and their descendants found them suitable as well for pickles and relishes. In Europe, they are most often simply parboiled and then sautéed in butter, or served with a cheese or cream sauce; elegant preparation calls for cutting them into small oval or "pigeon egg" shapes before cooking. In California, where they have become known as sunchokes, they are marinated in dressings and combined in a variety of "health" salads and used in place of water chestnuts in stir-fry dishes.

Jerusalem artichokes are often used without being peeled, but they require careful scrubbing to remove the dirt from the many crevices, which is best done with a stiff vegetable brush. If they are being pared before cooking, however, immediately after peeling, drop them into acidulated water (water with vinegar added, 1 teaspoon to each quart) to keep them from turning brown. The tubers are more easily peeled after they are boiled in salted water about 10 to 15 minutes, depending on size (overcooking makes them tough); they should then be dropped into cold water and scrubbed with a dish towel or scraped with a knife. For purées, cooked tubers may be forced through a sieve or mashed in a blender. Three-quarters of a pound of tubers makes about 1 cup of pulp.

Jerusalem artichokes are often recommended for diabetics and others whose sugar and starch intake must be limited, for the fresh tubers contain only sugar that can be assimilated by diabetics and almost no starch.

Jerusalem Artichokes with Mushrooms and Ham

INGREDIENTS
½ pound Jerusalem artichokes, well scrubbed
2 tablespoons olive oil
1 clove garlic, minced
½ pound mushrooms, sliced
1 cup cooked ham, diced
¼ teaspoon salt
⅛ teaspoon pepper
1 tablespoon chopped parsley

Drop Jerusalem artichokes into salted, boiling water and parboil for 10 minutes. Drain, peel, and cut into ¼-inch slices. Heat oil in a frying pan and sauté garlic and mushrooms over medium heat for about 5 minutes, stirring. Add sliced Jerusalem artichokes and sauté 5 minutes more. Add cooked ham, salt, and pepper, and mix well, continuing to sauté until ham is well heated. Sprinkle with parsley, mix well, and serve.
Serves 4.

Palestine Soup

"From this girasol we have made Jerusalem, and from the Jerusalem artichoke we make Palestine soup." (Thomas Love Peacock, Gryll Grange, 1861)

INGREDIENTS
2 tablespoons butter
1 onion, sliced
1½ pounds Jerusalem artichokes, peeled and sliced
4 cups chicken or veal stock
1 cup milk
¾ teaspoon salt
⅛ teaspoon white pepper

Garnish
chopped parsley
lemon slices

In a soup kettle, melt butter and sauté onion over low heat for 5 minutes or until it is translucent. Add the sliced Jerusalem artichokes, mix until they are well coated, and sauté over low heat for 5 minutes more. Add stock, bring to boil, and simmer half-covered for about 20 minutes or until artichokes are quite tender. Allow to cool and then purée in a blender or put through a sieve. Return purée to kettle, add milk, salt, and pepper, and heat thoroughly but do not boil. Serve immediately, garnished with chopped parsley and lemon slices.
Serves 6.

Beef with Snow Peas, Broccoli, and Sunchokes

INGREDIENTS
¼ cup vegetable oil
½ pound beef round or tenderloin, sliced into very thin strips
1 clove garlic, minced
2 cups broccoli, stems removed and separated into florets
1 cup beef broth

¼ pound snow peas, trimmed
1 cup firm Jerusalem artichokes, peeled and cut into ¼-inch slices
2 tablespoons cornstarch
1 tablespoon soy sauce
pinch of ground ginger

Garnish
¼ cup toasted almonds

Heat oil in a wok or large frying pan. Add sliced beef and garlic, stirring constantly until meat is well seared. Add broccoli and sauté for a minute, mixing, and then pour in broth. Cover and cook over low heat until broccoli is tender, about 10 minutes. Uncover and add snow peas and Jerusalem artichokes. In a bowl, blend cornstarch with ¼ cup of water, soy sauce, and ginger, and pour into wok or pan, stirring until liquid thickens. Garnish with almonds and serve with rice.
Serves 4.

Jerusalem Artichoke Pancakes

INGREDIENTS
1 pound Jerusalem artichokes, peeled and finely grated
1 egg, beaten well
2 tablespoons flour
½ teaspoon baking powder
¾ teaspoon salt
¼ teaspoon pepper
oil for frying

Press grated Jerusalem artichokes to remove any liquid and drain well. Combine artichokes in a bowl with beaten egg, flour, baking powder, salt, and pepper, and mix well. Drop by tablespoons into ½-inch hot oil and fry until well browned on both sides. Drain well on absorbent paper. Serve with sour cream.
Serves 4.

Jerusalem Artichoke Soufflé

INGREDIENTS
1 cup boiled and sieved Jerusalem artichokes
1 cup boiled and mashed potatoes
¼ cup milk
½ teaspoon salt
1 tablespoon butter
3 eggs, separated
1 scallion, finely sliced

Preheat oven to 400 degrees. Combine sieved Jerusalem artichokes and mashed potatoes with milk, salt, and butter in saucepan and cook over low heat, stirring constantly until mixture becomes a smooth purée. Remove from heat. Beat egg yolks into mixture, stir in scallion, and set aside. In a separate bowl, beat egg whites with a pinch of salt until stiff. Stir a large spoonful of beaten egg whites into mixture and gently fold in the remainder. Pour into greased 2-quart soufflé dish and place in middle of oven. Reduce heat to 375 degrees and bake without opening oven door for 45 minutes. Serve immediately.
Serves 4.

California Sunchoke Slaw

INGREDIENTS
¾ pound Jerusalem artichokes, peeled and coarsely grated
2 carrots, coarsely grated
2 scallions, finely sliced
2 tablespoons unsalted sunflower seeds
⅓ cup yogurt
1 tablespoon mayonnaise
1 tablespoon lemon juice
¼ teaspoon celery seeds

¼ teaspoon salt
⅛ teaspoon pepper

Combine grated Jerusalem artichokes and carrots in a bowl and mix together well. Sprinkle with scallions and sunflower seeds. In a separate bowl, combine yogurt, mayonnaise, and lemon juice and mix until smooth. Add celery seeds, salt, and pepper, mix, pour over slaw, and toss.
Serves 4.

Marinated Jerusalem Artichoke Salad

INGREDIENTS
1 pound Jerusalem artichokes, well scrubbed
3 scallions, sliced
¼ cup salad oil
2 tablespoons wine vinegar
2 tablespoons tomato juice
¼ teaspoon salt
⅛ teaspoon pepper

Garnish
2 tablespoons chopped parsley

Cook Jerusalem artichokes in salted boiling water until tender, about 15 minutes. Drain, peel, cut into ¼-inch slices, and allow to cool. Mix Jerusalem artichokes and scallions in a bowl. In a jar, combine oil, vinegar, tomato juice, salt, and pepper, cover tightly, and shake well to blend ingredients. Pour dressing over Jerusalem artichokes, mix, and allow to marinate several hours. Garnish with chopped parsley and serve.
Serves 4.

Jerusalem Artichoke Relish

INGREDIENTS
2 pounds Jerusalem artichokes, peeled and coarsely grated
3 sweet peppers, coarsely grated
3 medium onions, coarsely grated
6 teaspoons salt
1½ cups cider vinegar
½ cup sugar
1 teaspoon mustard seeds
½ teaspoon ground turmeric
¼ teaspoon dried red pepper flakes

Mix grated Jerusalem artichokes, peppers, and onions in bowl. Sprinkle with salt, mix, and let stand for several hours or overnight, weighted with a heavy pot or pan. Drain well, pressing out as much liquid as possible. In a large saucepan, mix vinegar, sugar, mustard seeds, turmeric, and pepper flakes, and bring to a boil. Add vegetable mixture, bring back to a boil, and boil for one minute. Pack in hot sterilized jars and seal immediately (see Appendix A, p. 138, for A Note on Preserving).
Makes approximately 5 half-pint jars.

Kale

"Kail in England simply expresses cabbage, but in Scotland represents the chief meal of the day. Hence the old-fashioned easy way of asking a friend to dinner was to ask him if he would take his kail with the family." Through this example, the noted dean of Edinburgh Edward Ramsay acquainted the readers of his *Reminiscences of Scottish Life & Character* (1861) with the significance of kale in his countrymen's diet. Served daily, traditionally in a hearty broth, this leafy green provided Scotland with subsistence for centuries; its ability to withstand all but the severest weather made it available throughout the winter in an age when other nutritious greens could not be imported fresh from warmer lands. Every family had its own patch of kale, and the rude enclosures attached to every country cottage became known as kailyards. This term was later associated with a school of Scottish poets and writers who at the end of the last century took up themes of rural life, writing sentimentally of a vanishing era. Perhaps more bitter associations with the realities of poverty—not just in Scotland but across the Continent—prompted many immigrants to America to relegate kale, no longer essential to their well-being, to a list of our most neglected vegetables.

Kale (also called borecole and cow cabbage) is a primitive form of cabbage of a kind that still grows wild in certain remote parts of Europe. Probably the first type of cabbage to have been cultivated—it appeared frequently on ancient Roman tables—kale is accurately described by its Latin name, *Brassica oleracea acephala*, as a garden cabbage that does not form a head (instead, its curly leaves grow off a central stalk). Identical in variety to collards (see Greens, Chapter 5), the two differ mainly in the form of their leaves and in their adaptability to temperature extremes, kale faring better in cooler climates.

HOW TO SELECT KALE

Kale is most plentiful in the fall and winter, and its flavor is said to be enhanced by frost, an idea that harks back to the Roman naturalist Pliny, who wrote in his *Natural History:* "In all kinds of Cabbages, hoarfrost contributes very materially to their sweetness." Whole plants of curly, deep bluish green leaves are usually picked for market, although in the home garden only the outer leaves are gathered, leaving each plant to continue to grow. Choose plants with crisp leaves of a dark color, avoiding those with yellowing leaves or wet decay spots. Kale wilts readily, but stored in a sealed plastic bag or closed container in the refrigerator, it will last for several days.

HOW TO PREPARE KALE

Kale is rarely eaten raw, for the leaves can be tough and sulfurous to the taste, but cooking yields a distinctly flavored, tender green and a wonderfully fresh country aroma. Any of the recipes used for spinach or other dark leafy greens—boiled, buttered, creamed, and so on—may be adapted for kale (see Greens, Chapter 5, Swiss Chard, Chapter 16). It seems, however, to have a particular affinity for potatoes, and this combination is often found in the traditional recipes of northern Europe.

Rinse kale thoroughly of any dirt clinging to the leaves, and remove the stalks and central ribs before cooking. The leaves are generally chopped or shredded and then boiled until tender, but they can be easily cooked with just the water that clings to them after washing, over low heat in a covered pan. This better preserves much of their high vitamin and mineral content. One pound of fresh kale will make about 6 cups when coarsely chopped and 2 to 3 cups when boiled or sautéed. The frozen kale sold in supermarkets can also be used in the following recipes.

Scotch Broth

INGREDIENTS
2 pounds meaty lamb bones
2 onions, sliced
1 carrot, diced
1 turnip, diced
1 teaspoon salt

½ cup barley, rinsed in cold water
½ pound kale, well washed and coarsely shredded
freshly ground pepper (to taste)

Place lamb bones, onions, carrot, turnip, salt, and barley in heavy kettle
with 2 quarts of water. Bring to a boil and skim off foam. Reduce heat,
cover, and simmer gently for about 1½ hours, or until meat is tender. If
broth is fatty, skim off excess from surface. Add washed and shredded
kale and simmer for a half-hour longer. Transfer lamb bones to dish and
remove meat from bones. Dice meat and return to soup. Add freshly
ground pepper to taste, and more salt if necessary. Serve hot.
Serves 6.

Caldo Verde

---

*Kale is a principal ingredient of the many versions of this traditional soup
prepared by the descendants of the early Portuguese settlers of New England.*

INGREDIENTS
4 potatoes, peeled and diced
1 pound kale, well washed and very finely shredded
2 teaspoons salt
¼ teaspoon pepper
3 tablespoons olive oil

Garnish
day-old French or Italian bread

Bring 2½ quarts water to a boil in a heavy kettle. Add potatoes and boil
gently for about 20 minutes or until they can be easily mashed. Remove
kettle from stove and mash potatoes well against side of kettle with fork
or wooden spoon (or remove potatoes from kettle with slotted spoon,
mash well in a separate bowl, and return to broth). Put kettle back on
stove, bring to a boil, and add finely shredded kale. Cover and cook over
moderate heat for 30 minutes or until tender. Stir in salt, pepper, and
oil, and serve hot in large soup bowls over chunks of crusty bread.
Serves 6.

Dutch Kale and Potato Stew (Stampot)

INGREDIENTS
2 pounds kale, well washed and finely chopped
2 pounds potatoes, peeled and cut into eighths
½ pound frankfurter or knockwurst
1 teaspoon salt
2 tablespoons butter

Boil kale in water until tender, about 30 minutes, and drain well. Arrange potatoes in a large kettle and add water until potatoes are half-covered. Add frankfurter or knockwurst and kale, sprinkle with salt, and cook uncovered over low heat until potatoes are very tender and mixture is dry (about 45 minutes). Remove frankfurter or knockwurst and cut into ¼-inch slices. Add butter to pot and mix well. Arrange potato-kale mixture on a platter with frankfurter slices on top.
Serves 6.

Kale and Eggs

INGREDIENTS
1 onion, chopped
3 tablespoons butter
1 pound kale, well washed and coarsely chopped
¼ teaspoon salt
4 eggs

Sauté onion in butter until golden. Add kale and salt and sauté covered for about 15 minutes or until tender. Beat eggs lightly and add to cooked kale, stirring until well mixed. Cook over moderate heat until eggs are set.
Serves 4.

Colcannon

This dish is traditionally served on Halloween in Ireland and Scotland, with a ring hidden in it predicting marriage for the maiden who finds it in her portion.

> *Did you ever eat colcannon when 'twas made with yellow cream,*
> *And the kale and praties blended like the picture in a dream?*
> *Did you ever take a forkful and dip it in the lake*
> *Of the clover-flavored butter that your mother used to make?*
> *Did you ever eat and eat, afraid you'd let the ring go past,*
> *And some old married sour-puss would get it at the last?*

INGREDIENTS
1 pound potatoes, peeled and diced
1 pound fresh kale, well washed and finely chopped
2 scallions, finely sliced
½ cup milk
1 teaspoon salt
¼ teaspoon pepper
2 tablespoons butter

Garnish
butter

In two separate saucepans, boil potatoes until they can be mashed (about 15 minutes) and kale until it is tender (about a half-hour). Drain potatoes and mash in saucepan until quite smooth. In a separate pan, simmer scallions in milk until soft and add to potatoes, beating well. Add well-drained boiled kale, season with salt and pepper, and beat over low heat. When mixture is smooth and hot, add 2 tablespoons butter, mix thoroughly, and serve immediately, garnishing each portion with more butter.
Serves 6.

Kale and Potato Sauté

INGREDIENTS
1 onion, chopped
3 tablespoons vegetable oil
1 pound potatoes, diced
1 pound kale, well washed and coarsely chopped
½ teaspoon salt
¼ teaspoon pepper

Sauté onion in oil in a large frying pan until golden. Add potatoes, kale, and salt and pepper, and sauté 5 minutes, stirring occasionally. Cover and simmer until tender, about 30 minutes.
Serves 6.

Kale with Anchovies

INGREDIENTS
1 pound kale, well washed and coarsely chopped
3 tablespoons olive oil
1 clove garlic
4 fillets of anchovy, diced
salt (to taste)
pepper (to taste)
juice of half lemon

Cook kale in boiling water until tender, about 30 minutes, and drain well. Heat oil in frying pan and sauté garlic until golden. Remove garlic and discard, add anchovies, and stir in well-drained, chopped kale. Cover and cook over moderate heat until kale is thoroughly heated. Add salt (if necessary) and pepper to taste and sprinkle with juice of half lemon. Serve hot.
Serves 4.

Mango

Just as the torrid heat of summer descends upon the vast expanse of India, the mango crop begins to ripen and the fruits take on their rosy blush. In the succeeding months, it seems that all India takes refreshment from their cooling, juicy flesh and that little else is eaten throughout the land. In the past, too, the spicy sweet taste of mangoes was much appreciated; they have been grown in India for at least four thousand and perhaps as much as six thousand years, which places them among the earliest cultivated fruits. The varieties of mango (*Mangifera indica*) exceed a thousand, and in a country in which more mangoes are grown than all other fruits combined, partisan tempers are known to flare in discussions over the particular merits of favored varieties. Groves of mangoes have their place in any description of this lush land, and they did as far back as the first millenium B.C., when they were frequently mentioned in such Sanskrit epics as the *Mahabharata* and the *Ramayana*. History, not literature, however, boasts of the greatest stand of mangoes; in the sixteenth century, the Mogul emperor Akbar the Great of Hindustan laid out an orchard that is said to have included one hundred thousand mango trees.

The Portuguese, who dominated trade with India during the sixteenth century, also appreciated the mango, and it was they who westernized the name *man-kay* ("fruit of the mango tree"), from the Tamil language of southern India. It was the Portuguese, too, who introduced the mango to Europe and brought it to the New World, where in the Caribbean today it is every bit as popular as it is in India.

HOW TO SELECT MANGOES

While numerous varieties of mangoes are known and cataloged, only a few different kinds find their way to American fruit stores. The major types seen here are round or kidney shape and about 6 inches long, in season from April through September. In addition, Puerto Rico exports a small, roundish mango in midsummer, at the height of its season on the island. Although mangoes are a spring and summer fruit, the many colors they turn when ripe—yellow, orange, red, and purple— are reminiscent more of autumn leaves. (One flat, kidney-shape variety, however, that is available here from winter into spring is ripe when it is all green or with just a blush of color. Only a slight softening of the fruit indicates its ripeness.) Choose fruits that are firm and still somewhat green, to be ripened at home at room temperature—some Indians ripen them in a jar of rice or wrapped in newspaper—or choose softer, yellowish-red ones to be used immediately; avoid fruits that seem mushy or withered. Mangoes can still be sweet and luscious with some black spotting on their skins. Fully ripe mangoes should be stored in the refrigerator until ready for use.

HOW TO PREPARE MANGOES

One commonly hears that when the British ruled India, they would retire to their bathtubs and enjoy ripe mangoes, and it is true that eating mangoes, though they are marvelously refreshing and tasty, especially when chilled, can be a challenge to one's table manners. Not only are mangoes extremely juicy, but they also have a large flat pit with hairs that tenaciously hold to the flesh around it. Because of the pit, mangoes cannot be cut in half. Instead, stand them on end and make a vertical slice on each side of the center, about ¾-inch apart. This will free most of the fruit into two manageable sections, leaving the orange flesh around the pit to be sucked on or cut away as best one can.

Mangoes are used in cooking in both their unripe and ripe stages. Unripe and half-ripe mangoes are widely known as the principal component of the preserved spicy chutneys and pickles made in India. Indeed, centuries ago, the word *mango* in English took on the secondary meaning of "pickle," so that one could speak of "cucumber mangoes" and "watermelon mangoes." Mango chows, jellies, and jams are made especially in the West Indies and Hawaii of half-ripe or ripe fruit. Ripe mangoes are made into stewed fruit, tarts, and pies, as well as purées for drinks, sauces, custards, soufflés, ices, and whips. Two cups of mango slices will make about 1 cup stewed and puréed fruit. Canned, sweetened mango purées are available in Hispanic and Indian markets.

Mango Curry

When a mango curry is included in an Indian meal, it is served as the last of the main dishes.

INGREDIENTS
3 tablespoons vegetable oil
1 onion, coarsely chopped
1 clove garlic, minced
1 teaspoon finely minced fresh ginger
¼ teaspoon ground coriander
¼ teaspoon cayenne
¼ teaspoon turmeric
¼ teaspoon ground cumin
3 green or half-ripe mangoes, peeled and cut into ¾-inch cubes
¼ teaspoon salt
2 tablespoons sugar

Heat oil in a heavy skillet over medium flame and fry onion, garlic, and ginger until onion begins to brown. Add coriander, cayenne, turmeric, and cumin and continue to fry for 5 minutes, stirring constantly. Add cubed mango, salt, and sugar, and mix until mango is well coated with spices. Add ¼ cup water, cover, reduce heat, and cook until mango is tender, about 15 to 30 minutes, depending on the ripeness of the mangoes. Serve over boiled rice.
Serves 4.

Mango Upside-down Cake

INGREDIENTS
½ cup butter, softened
½ cup brown sugar
2 cups ripe mango, peeled and cut into ¼-inch slices 3 inches in length
1½ cups flour
2 teaspoons baking powder
½ teaspoon salt
1 cup sugar
1 teaspoon vanilla
2 eggs, lightly beaten
⅔ cup milk

Preheat oven to 350 degrees. Melt ¼ cup butter in a 9-inch cast-iron skillet over low heat and remove from flame. Sprinkle bottom of pan with brown sugar and arrange mango slices side by side in skillet. Sift together flour, baking powder, and salt. In a separate bowl, cream the remaining ¼ cup softened butter with sugar until smooth and add vanilla and eggs and mix well. Combine with dry ingredients, alternating with milk, and beating until smooth after each addition. Pour batter over mango slices and bake in the oven about 45 minutes, until cake is well browned and a cake tester comes out clean. Allow to cool for 10 minutes and then invert carefully onto cake plate.
Makes 1 nine-inch skillet cake.

Caribbean Mango Fool

A fool, as its name suggests, is a light and fluffy confection, a dessert that is dearly loved by the British.

INGREDIENTS
2 cups ripe mango, peeled and sliced
¼ cup sugar
1 cup heavy cream

Garnish
nutmeg

Stew mangoes covered in ¼ cup water gently until very soft, about 15 to 20 minutes. Pass through a coarse sieve, pressing pulp with a wooden spoon. Flavor purée with sugar and mix well. Allow to cool and then chill thoroughly in the refrigerator for several hours. Whip cream until stiff and fold gently into mango purée. Spoon into dessert dishes, sprinkle with nutmeg, and serve immediately.

Serves 4.

Stewed Mangoes

"The most valuable tree, which has been introduced in Jamaica, in recent times, is the mangoe. . . . It has spread with great abundance, is dessert for the whites and food for the negros." (Sturge and Harvey, The West Indies in 1837)

INGREDIENTS
3 green or half-ripe mangoes, peeled and thinly sliced
1 cup sugar
¼ teaspoon cinnamon
¼ teaspoon allspice

Put mango slices, sugar, cinnamon, and allspice into a saucepan with water barely to cover. Bring to a boil and stew gently until mango is tender and syrup thickens, about 30 minutes.
Serves 4.

Mango Chutney

INGREDIENTS
6 cups unripe mango, peeled and cut into ½-inch cubes
1 large onion, coarsely chopped
½ cup seedless raisins
½ cup currants
2 tablespoons finely chopped fresh ginger
1 hot chili pepper, cored, seeded, and finely chopped
2 cloves garlic, finely chopped
2 teaspoons salt
1½ cups sugar
1½ cups vinegar

Combine mangoes with all other ingredients in a large enamel saucepan. Mix well and bring to a boil. Cook at slow boil about 1 hour or until sauce is brown and begins to thicken, and mangoes are tender but still intact. Ladle into hot sterilized jars, and seal immediately (see Appendix A, p. 138, for A Note on Preserving).
Makes approximately 6 half-pint jars.

Mango Sauce

INGREDIENTS
3 cups ripe mango, peeled and sliced
¼ cup sugar
2 tablespoons lemon or lime juice

Cook sliced mango gently in a covered saucepan, in ½ cup water until very soft, about 15 or 20 minutes. Remove from flame and put through a coarse sieve, pressing mango with the back of a wooden spoon. Return purée to saucepan, add sugar and lemon or lime juice, and cook gently, stirring occasionally, until the sauce begins to thicken. Serve hot or cold with French toast or sweet crepes, or over vanilla ice cream. Sauce will keep for a week or two in the refrigerator.
Makes approximately 1½ cups.

Mango Chow

Mango chows, ketchuplike "mixtures" popular in the islands of the Carib-bean, are probably based on East Indian chutneys and likewise may be served as a condiment with meats and curries.

INGREDIENTS
5 cups near-ripe mango, peeled and sliced thin
2 cups vinegar
1 onion, finely chopped
½ cup seedless raisins
½ cup currants
1 teaspoon ground ginger
½ teaspoon cinnamon
¼ teaspoon ground cloves
1 teaspoon salt
¼ teaspoon pepper
1 cup sugar

In a large enamel saucepan, combine sliced mangoes and 1 cup vinegar, bring to a boil, cover, and cook for about 20 minutes or until mangoes are quite soft. Allow to cool and pour through a coarse sieve, pressing softened mangoes through with a wooden spoon. Meanwhile, in a separate saucepan, combine onion, raisins and currants, ginger, cin-namon, cloves, salt, and pepper with the second cup of vinegar, bring to a boil, and simmer about 30 minutes. Return sieved mango to large saucepan, add sugar, and mix well. Pour in vinegar-raisin mixture, bring to a boil, and simmer about 30 minutes more, stirring occasionally with a wooden spoon, until the chow thickens like ketchup. Ladle into hot sterilized jars and seal immediately (see Appendix A, p. 138, for A Note on Preserving).
Makes approximately 4 half-pint jars.

Okra

Closely identified in America with the South, okra is a vegetable with a long history and strong culinary traditions on five continents. Native to north-central Africa—Ethiopia or the Sudan—this species of the mallow family (*Hibiscus esculentus*, or "edible hibiscus") was grown in the Nile Valley during the reign of the pharaohs, more than three thousand years ago. Slowly it was disseminated: south into the heart of the continent, where it was (and still is) used by countless African peoples; north and westward to the lands washed by the Mediterranean; and after the beginning of our era, eastward into India. The Balkans, southern France, and Spain all learned to cultivate okra, and over the centuries it also became distinctive in their cuisines.

Okra was first carried across the seas to the New World in the seventeenth century, and in 1756, the Englishman Patrick Browne was able to report in his *Civil and Natural History of Jamaica* that this transplant was the "principal ingredient in most of the soops, and pepper-pots, made in America; dishes frequently used in those parts of the world." The sailing ships that transported slaves to the West Indies and the Americas also brought okra from its native Africa, as well as the two names by which it is known today, *okra* and *gumbo*, both of which derive directly from West African tongues. Favored in plantation cooking throughout the South, okra was especially popular in the Louisiana Territory. There, as the common heritage of the French, Spanish, and African inhabitants of the Mississippi Delta, it was basic to creole cookery, and as *gumbo* gave its name to the characteristic thick stew of New Orleans as well as to a black jargon spoken there.

HOW TO SELECT OKRA

Okra is grown in the South, where it is available in markets year round; elsewhere it is most abundant from May through October, although it appears sporadically throughout the year. The tapered green

[65]

pods, which encase rows of white seeds, grow in ribbed and ribless varieties. They are best eaten young, when they are from 1 to 4 inches in length; although the smaller pods are most tender, larger ones are more convenient for slicing. Choose bright green, crisp pods that snap upon bending, avoiding those with discolorations or signs of shriveling or drying. Okra will keep for a week or two in the refrigerator (in the crisper or a closed plastic bag) before going limp and discoloring.

HOW TO PREPARE OKRA

The great variety of recipes reflects the extent and traditions of the countries in which okra has been grown and enjoyed. Simply, the young pods may be eaten raw (or after being blanched quickly and refreshed in cold water) in salads; boiled or steamed and served with butter; or, as is frequently done in the South, rolled in cornmeal and deep-fried. More elaborately, okra is married with tomatoes in all manner of dishes; it is stewed with meats or chicken or added to soups, which the gummy substance given off during extended cooking helps thicken.

Those who have had little experience with okra or who have tasted it under the worst circumstances regard it as a slimy and stringy vegetable, worthless in the kitchen except for adding to long-cooking soups and stews. When it is properly prepared, however, the mucilaginous property need not dominate. There is considerable disagreement, however, over correct methods for preparation. Some insist that okra be soaked in water before cooking, while others decry its touching water at all; some warn against cutting into the pod, while others instruct that it be sliced. Once it has been prepared for cooking by trimming off both ends of the pod, okra ought to be cooked rapidly, which should prevent it from getting slimy, whether soaked, sliced, or whole. (Frozen okra, cut or whole, works especially well in recipes for sautées, stews, and soups, but cooking times should be decreased.)

Indian Fried Okra with Garam Masala

INGREDIENTS
1 pound okra, trimmed and sliced into thin rounds
oil for frying

Garnish
salt
pepper
garam masala (recipe follows)

Heat enough oil for frying in a large frying pan or wok, and when it is hot, carefully drop in okra so that rounds form one layer. Fry until okra darkens and becomes crisp. Remove and drain on paper toweling. Continue to fry okra rounds in batches until all are cooked. Serve immediately, sprinkled with salt, pepper, and garam masala to taste.

Garam Masala
2 teaspoons cardamon seeds (removed from pods)
2 teaspoons whole cloves
2 teaspoons coriander seeds
2 sticks cinnamon, broken into pieces

Heat spices gently in a small skillet for 10 minutes, shaking occasionally to liberate the aromas. Mix in a blender until spices have been ground to a fine powder. Use as a flavoring. Garam masala will keep for months if it is stored in a dry, airtight container. It may also be bought prepared in Indian grocery stores.
Serves 4.

Bulgarian Okra Soup

INGREDIENTS
1 onion, finely chopped
3 tablespoons olive oil
2 teaspoons flour
1 pound baby okra, trimmed
1 teaspoon salt
1 teaspoon paprika
3 plum tomatoes, peeled and chopped
½ cup yogurt
1 egg
¼ teaspoon pepper

Sauté chopped onion in oil in heavy kettle until translucent. Sprinkle with flour and cook for 2 minutes, stirring constantly. Add okra, 3 cups hot water, salt, and paprika, and cook covered over medium heat without boiling for 20 minutes. Add tomatoes and continue cooking for another 10 minutes or until okra is tender.

While soup is cooking, pour yogurt into a tureen or serving bowl and beat in egg well. When soup is ready, pour into tureen over yogurt-egg mixture, stir, and season with pepper before serving.
Serves 4.

Seafood Gumbo

INGREDIENTS
2 onions, finely chopped
1 green pepper, finely chopped
2 stalks celery, finely chopped
3 tablespoons vegetable oil
3 tablespoons flour
1 sixteen-ounce can tomatoes, drained well and chopped
1 pound okra, trimmed and sliced into ½-inch rounds
1 clove garlic, minced
1½ teaspoons salt
¼ teaspoon pepper
dash cayenne
¼ teaspoon dried thyme
2 tablespoons parsley, chopped
1 bay leaf
4 small hard-shell crabs, rinsed in cold water, scalded, cleaned thoroughly, back shell removed, and quartered
1 pound shrimp, peeled and deveined
4 cups boiling water
1 dozen oysters, with their liquor

Sauté onions, green pepper, and celery in oil in deep heavy kettle until onions are translucent. Add flour and cook 5 minutes, stirring constantly. Add tomatoes, okra, garlic, salt, pepper, cayenne, thyme, parsley, bay leaf, crabs, and shrimp. Cover with 4 cups boiling water, mix well, and cook over low heat for 1½ hours. Add oysters with their liquor and cook 15 minutes longer. Serve in bowls over hot boiled rice. *Serves 6.*

North African Lamb Stew with Okra

INGREDIENTS
2 tablespoons vegetable oil
1½ pounds lean lamb, cut into 1-inch cubes
1 onion, chopped
2 cloves garlic, minced
½ teaspoon salt
¼ teaspoon pepper
¼ teaspoon turmeric
2 tablespoons chopped parsley
4 tomatoes, peeled and chopped (or 1 eight-ounce can tomatoes, drained well and chopped)
1 stick cinnamon
1 pound baby okra, trimmed (if large, cut into 1½-inch lengths)

Heat oil in heavy skillet and sauté lamb until lightly browned on all sides. Add onion, garlic, salt, pepper, turmeric, parsley, and tomatoes. Mix well and cook over medium heat for 5 minutes. Add ½ cup water and cinnamon stick and cook over gentle heat, covered, for 1 hour. Add okra, cover, and steam for a half-hour or until okra is tender.
Serves 4.

Quimbombó (Cuban Okra Stew)

INGREDIENTS
1 onion, finely chopped
1 small green pepper, finely chopped
4 tomatoes, chopped (or 1 eight-ounce can tomatoes,
   drained well and chopped)
1 clove garlic, minced
1 tablespoon oil
¼ pound cooked ham, cubed
1 cup chicken broth
bay leaf
salt (to taste)
pepper (to taste)
1 pound okra, trimmed and sliced into ½-inch rounds
1 tablespoon lemon juice

Garnish
plantain balls (see Plantain p. 94)

Prepare recipe for plantain balls. Meanwhile, in a kettle, fry onion, green pepper, tomatoes, and garlic in oil until soft. Add ham, broth, bay leaf, salt and pepper to taste, and cook slowly for 10 minutes. Add okra and cook until tender, about 20 minutes. Drop plantain balls into stew and cook covered for 5 minutes longer. Stir in lemon juice and serve as a vegetable with rice.
Serves 4.

Indian Sautéed Okra

INGREDIENTS
2 tablespoons vegetable oil
1 teaspoon black mustard seeds *
1 pound okra, trimmed
⅛ teaspoon turmeric
¼ teaspoon salt

---

* Available in Oriental groceries.

Heat oil in heavy skillet over medium flame. Add black mustard seeds and, when they begin to pop, add okra. Cover and cook for 10 minutes. Add turmeric and salt, mix well, and continue to cook, uncovered, stirring occasionally until okra is tender, about 15 minutes.
Serves 4.

Okra Foogath (African Stewed Okra)

INGREDIENTS
4 tablespoons oil
1 large onion, finely sliced
2 cloves garlic, minced
1 green chili pepper, chopped
¼ teaspoon cayenne
1 tablespoon chopped fresh ginger
1 pound okra, trimmed
½ teaspoon salt
1 tomato, thinly sliced

Heat oil in large, heavy skillet and sauté onion, garlic, chili pepper, cayenne, and ginger until onion is translucent. Add okra and salt, mix well, and sauté for 5 minutes, stirring once or twice. Add tomato and sauté another 2 minutes. Add ¼ cup water and simmer, covered, for about 15 minutes or until okra is tender.
Serves 4.

Limping Susan

The name of this rice pilaf, a favorite in Charleston, is a play on that of Hopping John, a well-known Southern specialty made of black-eyed peas and rice.

INGREDIENTS
4 slices bacon, diced
½ pound okra, trimmed and sliced into ½-inch rounds
1 cup raw long-grain rice
½ teaspoon salt

Fry bacon in kettle until crisp. Remove with a slotted spoon and reserve. Sauté okra in bacon fat over medium heat for 10 minutes. Add rice and salt and mix well with okra. Add 2 cups water, bring to a boil, cover, and cook over low heat for 30 minutes or until all water has been absorbed and rice is tender. Stir in bacon just before serving, and add more salt to taste if necessary.
Serves 4.

Spicy Pickled Okra

Allow these okra pickles to stand for several weeks before serving them on a relish tray or with meats.

INGREDIENTS
2 pounds okra, trimmed
5 cloves garlic, peeled
1¼ teaspoons red pepper flakes
3 cups vinegar
½ cup salt
1 tablespoon mustard seeds

Pack okra vertically into hot, sterilized canning jars. Add clove of garlic and ¼ teaspoon red pepper to each jar. Combine vinegar, 3 cups of water, salt, and mustard seeds in saucepan and bring to a boil. Pour over okra, and seal immediately (see Appendix A, p. 138, for A Note on Preserving).
Makes approximately 5 pint jars.

Greek Okra and Tomatoes

INGREDIENTS
2 tablespoons olive oil
1 pound okra, trimmed

juice of half lemon
1 onion, chopped
1 clove garlic, minced
2 tomatoes, peeled and diced
¼ cup parsley, chopped
½ teaspoon salt
¼ teaspoon pepper

Heat oil in heavy skillet over moderate heat and fry okra in batches until golden. Return okra to skillet and sprinkle with lemon juice. Add onion, garlic, tomatoes, and parsley, season with salt and pepper, and simmer, covered, over low heat until sauce thickens.
Serves 4.

Caribbean Cornmeal with Okra

INGREDIENTS
½ pound okra, trimmed and sliced into 1-inch lengths
1 cup cornmeal
1 onion, coarsely chopped
1 teaspoon salt

Garnish
butter
Tabasco sauce

Simmer okra, covered, in 1 cup water in a large saucepan for 15 minutes. Combine cornmeal, onion, and salt with 1 cup cold water and add to saucepan. Cook over medium heat, stirring often, until cornmeal thickens, about 20 minutes, making certain that cornmeal does not stick to bottom of pan. Serve garnished with pat of butter and Tabasco to taste.
Serves 4.

Papaya

Papayas and mangoes (Chapter 8)—fruits that grow side by side in tropical regions around the world—were not originally such close neighbors. Papayas are New World fruits, which were not seen by European eyes until the voyages of Columbus, while mangoes are natives of the East. It was not until the sixteenth and seventeenth centuries, when the new breed of global navigators carried these fruits and their seeds with them on their long voyages, that they began to be dispersed widely and grown in the same locales. At the time that mangoes were being brought westward to the Caribbean, papayas were being transported from America eastward, to Malaysia and India.

The Dutchman Jan Huyghen van Linschoten recapitulated the migration of the papaya in his much-translated *Voyage to the East Indies*, first published in English in 1598:

> There is also a fruite that came out of the Spanish Indies, brought from [beyond] ye Philippinas or Lusons to Malacca, & from thence to India, it is called Papaios, and is very like a Mellon. . . . This fruite at the first for the strangenes thereof was much esteemed, but now they account not of it.

And indeed the papaya spread so rapidly and took hold so easily in its new homes—later it was introduced to Hawaii and the Pacific islands, East Africa, China, and Japan—that when scientists began to chronicle the origin and history of plants, they thought that the papaya was a native of these other regions and had been imported into America.

The papaya (*Carica papaya*), also known as a tree melon, is sometimes incorrectly referred to as a pawpaw, which is actually the name of another American fruit, the custard apple. *Papaya* comes from the Spanish adaptation of *ababai*, its name in the language of the pre-Columbian peoples of the Caribbean, who were the first to enjoy this sweet tropical fruit.

HOW TO SELECT PAPAYAS

Papayas are sold throughout the year, though sporadically, but are at their height in the late spring and summer. They often appear in supermarkets and are plentiful in Hispanic groceries, Oriental markets, and health-food stores. The most common variety sold is the Solo papaya, grown commercially in Florida, California, and Hawaii; it is pear-shaped, has smooth skin, is about 6 inches in length, and weighs about 1 pound. Less common is a type of papaya that looks like a small watermelon and weighs several pounds or more. Solo papayas are usually green and unripe when they first reach the market, as they are picked early for ease of shipment. They will ripen readily at room temperature, turning yellow within a few days to a week. Choose fruits that are firm, avoiding those that are very soft or spotted. A ripe papaya should have a slight give when pressed gently, but its aroma is as good an index of its flavor, as is its color or tenderness. Ripe papayas will keep in the refrigerator a week or two.

HOW TO PREPARE PAPAYAS

Papayas have what is generally described as a musky flavor, which is a taste that takes some getting used to. But they are eaten with gusto in the tropics, where the sweet, orange flesh of fresh, ripe papayas, sprinkled with lemon or lime juice, is a favorite for breakfast. To enjoy papayas raw, cut them in half, scoop out the slippery, black, pepper-cornlike seeds, and eat like a melon; or peel, slice, or purée them in a blender, depending on the recipe.

Both ripe and unripe papayas can be cooked. Ripe, they are used in desserts, puréed for sauces, ices, and ice creams. (One papaya will yield about a cup of blended pulp.) Unripe, papayas are treated like squash—steamed, boiled, baked, sautéed, and stuffed. And they are also made into relishes, pickles and chutneys. Unripe papayas are typically sautéed or stewed with meats and poultry, which they tenderize, owing to the presence of the enzyme papain. This enzyme is the principal ingredient in many commercial meat tenderizers, but its use has been known throughout the ages wherever papayas are grown.

Lamb Curry with Mashed Papaya

INGREDIENTS
3 tablespoons vegetable oil
¼ teaspoon black mustard seeds *
1 onion, coarsely chopped
1 clove garlic, minced
1 teaspoon finely minced fresh ginger
1 fresh hot chili pepper, finely chopped
1½ pounds lamb, cut into ½-inch cubes
½ teaspoon ground cumin
¼ teaspoon turmeric
¼ teaspoon ground coriander
½ teaspoon salt
¾ cup unripe or half-ripe papaya pulp (blended)
juice of half lemon

Garnish
2 tablespoons chopped fresh coriander *

Heat oil over medium flame in a large frying pan and add mustard seeds, onion, garlic, ginger, and chili pepper. Fry until onion is brown. Add cubed lamb, cumin, turmeric, coriander, and salt, and cook over high heat until meat is brown on all sides. Add papaya pulp, mix well, cover, and cook over medium heat until meat is done, about 45 minutes to an hour. Sprinkle with lemon juice, garnish with chopped coriander, and serve with rice.
Serves 4.

* Available in Oriental groceries.

Chicken with Papaya

INGREDIENTS
1 clove garlic, cut in half
2 tablespoons vegetable oil
1 2½- to 3-pound chicken, cut into 8 pieces
1 large onion, coarsely chopped
½ teaspoon salt
¼ teaspoon pepper
½ cup chicken broth
1 unripe or half-ripe papaya, peeled and cut into 1-inch cubes

Cook garlic halves in oil in a large skillet until golden, then remove and discard. Add the chicken pieces to the hot oil, skin side down, and cook until brown; turn and brown on other side. Add onion, mix well to coat with oil, and cook 5 minutes. Add salt, pepper, and chicken broth; cover and cook over low heat for 30 minutes. Add papaya pieces to pan, mix, return lid, and cook until papaya and chicken are tender, about 20 minutes more. Serve with rice.
Serves 4.

Hawaiian Papaya Pickle

INGREDIENTS
4 cups unripe or half-ripe papaya, peeled and cut into 1-inch cubes
1 cup vinegar
2 cups sugar
½ teaspoon whole cloves
½ teaspoon whole peppercorns
2 bay leaves

Put cubed papaya into a kettle with water to cover, bring to a boil, cover, and simmer until papaya becomes tender, about 20 minutes.

Meanwhile, combine vinegar and sugar with ½ cup water in a large saucepan and heat over low flame, stirring until sugar dissolves. Add cloves, peppercorns, and bay leaves and simmer for 15 minutes. Add drained, cooked papaya and simmer gently until papaya becomes translucent—about 20 to 30 minutes. Remove papaya from liquid with slotted spoon and fill hot sterilized jars. Bring syrup back to boil and strain into jars over papaya and seal immediately (see Appendix A, p. 138, for A Note on Preserving).
Makes approximately 4 half-pint jars.

Papaya Bread

INGREDIENTS
3 eggs
¾ cup oil
1½ cups sugar
2 cups unripe papaya, coarsely shredded
2 teaspoons grated orange rind
½ teaspoon vanilla
3 cups sifted flour
¾ teaspoon salt
½ teaspoon cinnamon
½ teaspoon ground ginger
2 teaspoons baking powder
1 teaspoon baking soda
1 cup chopped walnuts or pecans

Preheat oven to 350 degrees. Beat eggs until frothy and add oil gradually, beating constantly. Add sugar and beat hard until creamy and light. Stir in shredded papaya, orange rind, and vanilla. In a separate bowl, combine flour with salt, cinnamon, ginger, baking powder, and baking soda and stir into papaya mixture, one cup at a time, beating well after each addition. Fold in nuts and pour into well-greased 9-inch loaf pan. Bake until bread pulls away from side and is nicely browned, about an hour.
Makes 1 nine-inch loaf.

Baked Papaya

INGREDIENTS
2 firm ripe papayas, cut in half, seeds removed
2 teaspoons brown sugar
¼ teaspoon cinnamon
2 tablespoons butter
2 teaspoons lemon juice

Preheat oven to 325 degrees. Sprinkle papaya halves with brown sugar and cinnamon and arrange in buttered baking dish. Dot with butter and sprinkle with lemon juice and bake for about a half-hour or until papaya is soft. Serve as a vegetable with turkey or roasts.
Serves 4.

Fresh Papaya Relish

INGREDIENTS
1 ripe papaya, peeled and cut into ½-inch cubes
1 teaspoon finely minced fresh hot chili pepper
¼ teaspoon salt
juice of half lemon or lime

Combine cubed papaya with chili pepper, salt, and lemon or lime juice and mix well. Allow to marinate for a half-hour. Serve with pork or chicken, or with curries.
Serves 4.

Papaya Sherbet

INGREDIENTS
1½ cups ripe papaya pulp (blended)
¼ cup orange juice
2 tablespoons lemon juice
½ cup sugar
¾ cup milk

Combine papaya pulp with orange and lemon juice. Stir sugar into milk and gradually combine with papaya mixture, mixing until smooth. Pour mixture into two freezer trays and put in freezer. After a half-hour, when mixture has become solid around the edges of the trays, remove from freezer, empty into bowl and beat until smooth. Return to trays, place in freezer, and after a half-hour, repeat process. Then allow sherbet to freeze for several hours until hard. Thaw slightly before serving.
Serves 4.

Persimmon

"Lushious sweet"—thus did Thomas Herriot tantalize his English compatriots with news of the American persimmon, one of the riches he enjoyed on his 1585 visit to Virginia in the company of Sir Walter Raleigh. Other Europeans soon echoed his praises, but they also pointed out, as Captain John Smith of Jamestown did in 1612, that "if it be not ripe it will drawe a mans mouth awrie with much torment; but when it is ripe, it is as delicious as an Apricock." This bountiful fall fruit was for some early settlers their only source of sweetness: From the Indians, they learned to savor persimmons cooked into puddings and made into syrups. Smith reported also that the Indians "preserve them as Pruines," calling them "Putchamins," his spelling of the Algonquian name, which translates as "dried fruit." Its botanical name, *Diospyros*, meaning "divine food," aptly suggests the pleasure that generations of Americans have taken from this fruit.

The round, maroon persimmon that our forebears enjoyed (*Diospyros virginiana*) is now encountered mainly in the wild or on old farms. The round or plum-shape bright orange varieties sold commercially are not native to America. Originally from China and then Japan, they were introduced here soon after Commodore Perry's intrusion into Japan in 1852. Now, these persimmons (*Diospyros kaki*—"kaki" being their name in Japanese) are grown in orchards in California, Louisiana, and Florida; in the Mediterranean, they thrive in Spain, southern France, Italy, and North Africa. While persimmons have had a long history in America, their continued popularity is due not so much to the descendants of the first settlers as to more recent immigrants from Europe, especially Italians, whose taste for the sweet *cachi* of their homeland has kept this luscious fruit available in the markets of this country.

HOW TO SELECT PERSIMMONS

These bright, red-orange fruits, 2 to 4 inches in diameter, come to market late in October, about the time of the first frost, and are plentiful until the end of the year. Plum-shape persimmons, the most common variety, must be very soft and pulpy when eaten. Generally they are picked and marketed when hard—ripe persimmons require delicate handling—but they will ripen readily at room temperature. Ripening can be speeded by putting persimmons in a tightly closed plastic bag, and folklore or chemistry has it that an apple added to the bag will enhance the process. Avoid fruits that have dark bruises or split skins, but do not hesitate to buy them when they are very soft—almost like nectar encased in a skin—for this is when they are sweetest. Completely to the contrary, the round variety now beginning to be sold more widely should be bought and eaten when they are still somewhat firm or only slightly soft. To enjoy persimmons in off-seasons, simply put them in an airtight container in the freezer, where they will keep for many months.

HOW TO PREPARE PERSIMMONS

Although persimmons have a rich culinary tradition, no recipe can rival the sweet pleasure of a ripe persimmon eaten plain. When the leafy cap is cut off and the fruit split lengthwise, the inside glistens with a delicate, slippery-smooth, red-orange pulp that tastes unlike any common fruit. (Some persimmons will have a few black, elongated seeds, similar in appearance to small date pits, which should be removed.) Persimmons can be eaten with a spoon like a melon, or, somewhat messily, sucked out of the skin. They can also easily be sieved or blended and served as a naturally sweetened dessert, eaten like a custard or used in baking. Frozen, they can be enjoyed as a simple sweet ice, or, as served in France, sprinkled with liqueur, and can easily be blended into a frothy purée. Two medium persimmons make about a cup of purée.

Persimmons are featured in Southern cookery, especially in Virginia, and in the Midwest, where puréed persimmon is made into pies, puddings, cakes, breads, chiffons, and ices. The spices traditionally used with persimmon include cinnamon, nutmeg, mace, and ginger, but only a light touch from the spice shelf will allow the delicate flavor of the cooked fruit to come through.

Wholesome Persimmon Pudding

INGREDIENTS
1 cup persimmon pulp (sieved or blended)
¼ cup light honey
1 cup whole wheat pastry flour
¼ teaspoon cinnamon
1 teaspoon baking soda
1 cup milk
1 egg, lightly beaten
1 teaspoon vanilla
½ cup seedless raisins

Preheat oven to 325 degrees. In a bowl, combine persimmon pulp and honey. Mix together flour, cinnamon, and baking soda and add to bowl, beating well with the persimmon-honey mixture. In a separate bowl, combine milk, beaten egg, and vanilla and stir into batter, beating well. Fold in raisins and turn into well-buttered 1-quart soufflé or baking dish and bake slowly until pudding pulls off side of dish, about 1½ hours. The pudding will be moist when done. Serve warm with whipped cream, hard sauce, or vanilla ice cream.
Serves 4.

Persimmon Nut Cookies

INGREDIENTS
½ cup butter, softened
1 cup sugar
1 egg, lightly beaten
1 cup persimmon pulp (sieved or blended)
2 cups flour

1 teaspoon baking soda
½ teaspoon cinnamon
½ teaspoon nutmeg
⅛ teaspoon salt
1 cup pecans or walnuts, broken into pieces

Preheat oven to 350 degrees. Cream softened butter and sugar and beat until well blended. Beat in egg and then add persimmon pulp. In a separate bowl, sift together flour, baking soda, cinnamon, nutmeg, and salt, and gradually add to persimmon mixture, blending well as it is added. Stir in nut pieces and drop by teaspoonfuls onto greased cookie sheets. Bake about 12 to 15 minutes, until these rather thick cookies are well browned and a cake tester comes out clean.
Makes 3 dozen cookies.

Persimmon Whipped Cream Pie

INGREDIENTS
1 nine-inch sweet pie crust, baked (see Appendix B, p. 140)
2 cups persimmon pulp (sieved or blended)
2 tablespoons orange juice or orange liqueur
1 cup heavy cream

Garnish
¼ persimmon, frozen

Prepare and bake pie crust. Meanwhile, combine persimmon pulp and orange juice or liqueur in a bowl. In a separate bowl, whip heavy cream until stiff and fold into the persimmon pulp. Turn into a baked pie shell and chill for at least an hour. Remove from refrigerator, garnish with thin slices of persimmon, which can be easily cut when the fruit is frozen, and serve.
Makes 1 nine-inch pie.

Persimmon Cream Cheese Frosting

INGREDIENTS
4 ounces cream cheese, softened
3 tablespoons persimmon pulp (sieved or blended)
1 teaspoon lemon juice
¾ cup sifted confectioner's sugar
¼ cup finely chopped nuts

In a bowl, cream softened cream cheese until fluffy. Add persimmon pulp and lemon juice and beat until smooth and well blended. Blend in the confectioner's sugar gradually until the frosting is of a good consistency for spreading, adding more sugar if necessary. Stir in chopped nuts and spread on cake or cupcakes.
Ices one 9 × 13-inch cake.

Persimmon Bread

INGREDIENTS
2 cups flour
1½ teaspoons baking soda
1½ teaspoons baking powder
½ teaspoon salt
½ cup sugar
¼ pound butter, softened
2 eggs, lightly beaten
2 cups persimmon pulp (sieved or blended)
1 cup chopped walnuts or pecans

Preheat oven to 350 degrees. Sift together flour, baking soda, baking powder, and salt. In a separate bowl, cream sugar and butter until smooth and beat in eggs. Add to dry ingredients, alternating with persimmon pulp, and mix well. Fold in chopped nuts and turn batter into a greased 9-inch loaf pan. Bake for about an hour, until bread is dark brown and cake tester comes out clean.
Makes 1 nine-inch loaf.

Persimmon Butter

INGREDIENTS
4 cups persimmon pulp (sieved or blended)
2 cups sugar
3 tablespoons lemon juice
¼ teaspoon cinnamon

In a deep kettle, combine persimmon pulp, sugar, lemon juice, and cinnamon and cook slowly over low heat, uncovered, stirring occasionally, until mixture is thick enough to spread, about 30 to 45 minutes. Ladle into hot, sterilized jars and seal immediately (see Appendix A, p. 138, for A Note on Preserving).
Makes 4 half-pint jars.

Plantain

In every region, or culture, one food—commonly rice, corn, potatoes, breadstuffs, or beans—forms the staple on which humanity survives. To a substantial number of people living in moist, tropical regions, the plantain is such a food. A member of the banana family that is eaten only when cooked, the plantain is easy to grow and abundant all year round. It is high in food value, easily digested, and versatile—"the relief of all poverty," according to the Spanish missionary José Gumilla, writing in the mid-eighteenth century. "In America they serve as bread, as meat, as drink, as conserve and everything else, because they satisfy hunger in all these ways." The Spanish and Portuguese introduced plantains and bananas to the New World (seventeenth- and eighteenth-century descriptions of tropical America do not generally distinguish between them). From the lands of their origin, the far reaches of India and Malaysia, they were transported to the Canary Islands and Africa. From there, plantains spread eastward, and by the seventeenth century, it could be said that plantain cultivation had encircled the earth.

The large, broad, flat leaves of the plantain tree—its name comes from the Spanish *plátano*, or "flat"—gave rise to the popular conception that this was the fig that grew in the Garden of Eden: Adam and Eve had tasted of the forbidden fruit, "and they knew that they were naked; and they sewed fig leaves together and made themselves aprons" (Genesis 3:7). Others believed that the plantain itself was the Tree of Knowledge. Because of these legends, the plantain was known variously as Adam's fig or Adam's apple; both names had been current for hundreds of years by the time the plantain was given its botanical name, *Musa paradisiaca*, or "fruit of Paradise."

HOW TO SELECT PLANTAINS

Plantains are widely available throughout the year in markets that serve Hispanic communities, and they can often be found in supermarkets as well. They resemble bananas but are generally larger and harder and are sold individually rather than in bunches. Plantains have three or four clearly defined sides, compared to the more usual four- or five-sided but less distinct shape of the banana. They are usually shipped to market in their unripe state, with completely green skins, but since they are used in various states of maturity, they can be bought green, yellow, brown, and even when the skin is almost totally black. Plantain skin is tougher and more protective than a banana's, and the flesh is usually unaffected even when the skin is highly blemished. Plantain recipes specify the degree of ripeness required, but if one is not sure how they will be used, it is best to buy plantains at their greenest stage and allow them to ripen slowly at home. Stored at room temperature, green plantains should become a full yellow-brown within a week and turn black by the next. If they are kept wrapped in paper, the plantains should remain green for a longer time.

HOW TO PREPARE PLANTAINS

Even when very ripe, plantains are not eaten raw. They are cooked in tropical regions on both sides of the Atlantic similarly, in an endless variety ranging from popular fried street snacks to stews, mashed vegetables, and desserts. Green, starchy plantains are rather bland, not unlike a mealy potato; half-ripe yellow and ripe brown plantains somewhat resemble sweet potatoes; and overripe black-skinned ones have the flavor of bananas. Plantains are cooked simply—baked or roasted in their skins, boiled and mashed, sautéed, or deep-fried (twice) into chips. They also are grated and added to soups as a thickener, combined in soups and stews with other vegetables and meat, and fried gently in syrup or baked in desserts.

Although plantains resemble bananas, they require greater dexterity in peeling. First cut off both ends and slice the fruit in half crosswise. Then with a sharp knife, score the skin lengthwise along the ridges and carefully peel it away with the fingers sideways, rather than lengthwise as one does with a banana.

Fried Plantain Cubes

A spicy dish served as a snack in West Africa.

INGREDIENTS
1 onion, finely chopped
1 teaspoon finely minced fresh ginger
1 teaspoon salt
¼ teaspoon cayenne
2 overripe (black) plantains, peeled and cubed
vegetable oil for frying

Combine onion, ginger, salt, and cayenne in a bowl. Add plantain cubes and mix until plantains are well coated. Heat about ½-inch oil in a heavy skillet until it is quite hot and fry plantain cubes until they are brown on all sides. Drain on paper towels and serve as a snack or hors d'oeuvre.
Serves 4.

Garlic Soup with Plantain Balls

INGREDIENTS
1 tablespoon olive oil
2 cloves garlic
6 cups clear chicken broth
1 unripe (green) plantain, peeled and sliced crosswise into ¼-inch pieces

Heat oil in a saucepan and sauté garlic cloves gently until soft. Remove garlic and add broth and bring to a boil. Drop in plantain slices and cook at a slow boil until soft, about 20 minutes. Remove plantain slices with a slotted spoon, drain, and mash in a bowl until smooth. Form into 1-inch balls and drop back into heated broth; cover and simmer 5 minutes longer.
Serves 4.

Plantain Balls

"Having brought the fruit home to their own houses, and pulling off the skin of so much as they will use, they boil it in water, making it into balls, and so they eat it." (P. A. Ligon, A True and Exact History of the Island of Barbadoes, 1673)

INGREDIENTS
1 unripe (green) plantain, peeled and sliced crosswise into ¼-inch pieces
½ teaspoon salt

Cook plantain slices in a pot of unsalted boiling water until they are quite soft, about 20 minutes. Drain and mash until very smooth. Season with salt and form into balls about an inch in diameter. Plantain balls may be simmered covered for about 5 minutes in soup, steamed and served as a vegetable, or added to traditional Latin American stews or "creole" soups, such as quimbombó (see Okra p. 70).
Serves 4.

Caribbean Stew with Plantains

This soupy stew (sancocho) *is one of many typical stews of the Caribbean, Central America, and northern South America that are made with both green and ripe plantains.*

INGREDIENTS
1 pound stewing beef, cut into 1-inch cubes
1 pound lean pork, cut into 1-inch cubes
1 onion, coarsely chopped
2 cloves garlic, chopped
2 green peppers, chopped
2 tomatoes, chopped
1 pound yauzia (yucca),* peeled and cut into 1-inch cubes

1½ teaspoons salt
¼ teaspoon pepper
3 sprigs parsley
½ pound calabaza * (or winter squash), peeled
  and cut into 1-inch cubes
½ pound yams, peeled and cut into 1-inch cubes
2 unripe (green) plantains, peeled and sliced
  crosswise into ½-inch pieces
2 half-ripe or ripe (yellow or brown) plantains,
  peeled and sliced crosswise into ½-inch pieces

Put beef and pork in a large kettle and cover with 8 cups of water. Bring to a boil and skim off foam. Reduce heat and add onion, garlic, green peppers, tomatoes, yauzia, salt, pepper, and parsley, and simmer for half-hour. Add calabaza (or squash), yams, and green plantains and simmer half-hour longer, or until vegetables are tender. Add ripe plantains and cook until they are tender, about 20 minutes. Serve in large soup bowls.
Serves 8.

* Available in Hispanic groceries.

Bengali Stewed Vegetables with Plantains

Serve this traditional homestyle stew (jhol) from India over rice. A heartier dish can be made by adding slices of fish fillets (sautéed in oil until well browned) just before serving.

INGREDIENTS
3 tablespoons vegetable oil
2 teaspoon cumin seeds
1 large potato, cut into ¾-inch cubes
1 unripe (green) plantain, peeled and sliced crosswise into ¼-inch pieces
1 small eggplant, unpeeled, cut into ¾-inch cubes
3 large outer leaves of cabbage, roughly torn into 2-inch pieces
1 zucchini, cut into ½-inch slices

½ teaspoon ground turmeric
½ teaspoon ground cumin
¼ teaspoon ground pepper
¾ teaspoon salt
1 tomato, chopped

Garnish
lemon wedges

Heat oil in large frying pan, add cumin seeds, and fry until they become aromatic and darken. Add vegetables successively according to the length of time they require for cooking: first potato, then plantain, eggplant, and cabbage leaves, stirring so that they are well coated with oil. Cook each for about 2 minutes before adding the next vegetable. Add zucchini, turmeric, ground cumin, pepper, and salt, and 1½ cups water and mix well. Cover and cook 10 minutes. Add chopped tomato, cover, and cook until vegetables are tender but not mushy, about 5 to 10 minutes. Garnish with lemon wedges and serve with rice.
Serves 4.

Puerto Rican Plantain-Meat Omelette (Piñon)

INGREDIENTS
4 ripe (brown) plantains, peeled, sliced in half lengthwise and crosswise into 2-inch pieces
vegetable oil for frying
1 pound ground pork
1 onion, finely chopped
1 cup chopped ripe tomatoes (or 1 eight-ounce can tomatoes, drained well and chopped)
½ green pepper, finely chopped
1 pound green beans, cut into 1-inch lengths
2 tablespoons chopped green olives
1 tablespoon chopped capers

¾ teaspoon salt
¼ teaspoon pepper
6 eggs, beaten well

Preheat oven to 350 degrees. In a large, oven-proof frying pan, sauté plantain slices in ¼-cup vegetable oil over medium heat in two batches until golden, adding more oil as necessary for second batch. Remove plantains and drain on paper towels. In same pan sauté ground pork, onion, tomatoes, and green pepper over medium heat for about 15 minutes, until meat is well browned. Transfer meat mixture to a large bowl and add green beans, which have been boiled or steamed until just tender (about 10 minutes), olives, capers, salt, and pepper, and mix well. Put 2 tablespoons of oil in frying pan and heat slowly. Pour in half the beaten eggs and while the eggs begin to cook arrange plantains in a layer in pan. Layer the meat mixture on top of the plantains, add the remaining plantains on top of the meat, and pour in remaining eggs. Transfer frying pan to oven and bake until eggs are well set, about 15 minutes.
Serves 6.

Plantain Omelette

INGREDIENTS
1 ripe (brown) plantain, peeled and sliced crosswise
    into ½-inch pieces
2 tablespoons vegetable oil
4 eggs, beaten well
¼ teaspoon salt

In a 10-inch frying pan, sauté plantain slices in 2 tablespoons oil over medium heat until golden, adding additional oil if necessary. Remove from pan and drain on paper towels. Add salt to the beaten eggs, mix, and pour into frying pan. Add browned plantain slices and cook until eggs are set on bottom. Slide omelette onto a plate and invert it back into pan. Cook for another minute, until bottom is done.
Serves 2.

Twice-Fried Plantains

This is the traditional method for making tostones, crispy fried plantains served throughout Latin America to accompany stews and meat and fish dishes.

INGREDIENTS
2 unripe (green) plantains, peeled and sliced diagonally
   into long ½-inch-thick pieces
oil for deep frying
salt

Drop diagonally sliced pieces of plantain into iced salted water and let stand about a half-hour. Remove plantains, drain, pat dry, and carefully drop in batches into deep hot fat. Fry until plantain slices are tender and lightly browned on both sides—about 5 minutes. Remove slices with slotted spoon, drain on paper towels, and then flatten with back of spatula or with palm of hand covered by towels. Dip into iced salted water, drain, and fry again in hot oil until golden brown and crisp. Drain on paper towels, sprinkle with salt to taste, and serve.
Serves 4.

Mashed Plantains

In Africa and the Caribbean, plantains are made into a thick mush known as fou-fou.

INGREDIENTS
3 unripe (green) plantains, peeled and sliced crosswise
   into ½-inch pieces
1½ teaspoons salt
2 tablespoons butter

Garnish
butter

Cook plantain slices in a pot of unsalted boiling water until quite soft—about 20 minutes. Drain and mash plantains in a bowl with a potato masher or fork until very smooth. Add salt and butter, reheat, and serve like mashed potatoes, garnished with large pat of butter.
Serves 4.

Plantains in Syrup

While plantains in syrup make a fine dessert, they are also served in Cuba as a side dish with meats or beans and rice.

INGREDIENTS
4 overripe (black) plantains, carefully peeled and cut in half crosswise
4 tablespoons butter
¼ cup sugar
1 teaspoon cinnamon

Fry plantains in butter over low heat in an enamel frying pan until golden all over, turning them gently. Remove from pan. Add sugar and cinnamon to pan with ¼ cup hot water and stir to mix well. Return plantains to frying pan and cook slowly, turning them occasionally until syrup begins to thicken.
Serves 4.

Pomegranate

Anyone who has ever cut open a pomegranate and seen the profusion of translucent reddish seeds will immediately understand why this sumptuous fruit became a symbol of fertility throughout the ancient world. The pomegranate seems to have originated in western Asia, but it was cultivated in the earliest civilizations and was soon known from the Indus Valley to the western reaches of the Mediterranean. Within the fulsome imagery of the Song of Songs, references to pomegranate orchards are found: "Let us go out early to the vineyards, and see whether the vines have budded, whether the grape blossoms have opened and the pomegranates are in bloom. There I will give you my love" (7:12). The Romans imported the pomegranate from North Africa, calling it *malum punicum*, or "apple of Carthage," while the name *pomegranate* derives from the Latin *pomum granatum*, or "seeded apple." Both terms are combined in its botanical nomenclature, *Punica granatum*.

In ancient Greece, the fruitful pomegranate and the endless cycle of the seasons were clearly linked by the story of Persephone. According to the myth, Persephone's mother Demeter was so grieved over the abduction of her daughter by Pluto, god of the underworld, that she withdrew fertility from the earth. Zeus intervened, promising to restore Persephone to her mother, but on the condition that she had eaten nothing in the nether regions. Unfortunately, Persephone had quenched her thirst with the juice of several pomegranate seeds and thus was sentenced to spend an equivalent number of months each year with Pluto, during which time the earth would be without vegetation. A renewal of life would come only on her return each spring. It was this association of the pomegranate with death and rebirth that later made this fruit a Christian symbol of the Resurrection.

HOW TO SELECT POMEGRANATES

Mature pomegranates are about the size of large oranges, with hard skins enclosing clusters of pulpy seeds that have the appearance of bright red corn kernels. Pomegranates are usually picked somewhat before they are fully ripe but generally are ready to be eaten when they appear in the market, from early fall through mid-winter. Select fruit with skin that is firm, without splits, and of a good, deep red color. Pomegranates can be stored in the refrigerator for several weeks.

HOW TO PREPARE POMEGRANATES

Pomegranates figure in the traditional cooking of eastern Europe, the Near East, and northern India, as well as Spain and Latin America. The acid-sweet juice is frequently used as a marinade for meats, as a substitute for stock or bouillon in soups and stews, and as a basis for sauces, drinks, and syrups (grenadine, for one). The seeds are usually eaten out of hand, fresh from the fruit, and they also make an interesting addition to salads and an unusual garnish.

Eating the seeds from a pomegranate is messy. There is no tried-and-true method of getting at the seeds without squirting the deep-red juice all over. One way to minimize stains is to slice off the top of the fruit above the seeds and score the skin into segments, thus allowing the skin to be peeled back from the complete fruit and the seeds to be separated in their natural clusters.

Extracting the juice of a pomegranate is simply done by cutting the fruit into quarters and squeezing it in a pressure citrus juicer (it is best to avoid rotating juicers). Depending on their size, two or three fruits will yield a cup of juice. Canned or bottled pomegranate juice may be substituted for fresh in the following recipes.

Eggplant Appetizer

Pomegranate juice elaborates this typical eggplant appetizer as made in the Georgian region of the Soviet Union.

INGREDIENTS
1 large eggplant

1 clove garlic, minced
3 tablespoons olive oil
¼ cup pomegranate juice
1 tablespoon lemon juice
½ teaspoon salt
¼ teaspoon sugar
⅛ teaspoon black pepper

Garnish
1 tablespoon pomegranate seeds

Grill whole eggplant over charcoal fire or bake on cookie sheet in 400-degree oven until it is very soft, about 30 to 45 minutes. Remove from heat and allow to cool. Peel eggplant into bowl, discarding skin and pouring off any liquid. Mash with back of wooden spoon. Add garlic, oil, pomegranate juice, lemon juice, salt, sugar, and pepper, and mix well. Let mixture set for a half-hour before serving at room temperature, garnished with pomegranate seeds.
Serves 4.

Pomegranate Syrup

This syrup is the basis for many Armenian and Persian dishes. It is served as an accompaniment to roast or barbecued lamb, pork, or chicken, with fish, or over fried eggplant. Diluted with water or soda and served over ice, it makes a refreshing summer drink.

INGREDIENTS
2 cups pomegranate juice
1 cup sugar

Heat juice over medium heat in heavy enamel saucepan. Add sugar, stirring constantly with wooden spoon until dissolved. Cook over medium heat for about 20 minutes or until liquid begins to thicken or become syrupy. May be served hot or cold.
Makes approximately 2 cups.

Persian Pomegranate Soup

INGREDIENTS
1 onion, sliced
2 tablespoons butter
½ cup lentils
½ cup rice
½ cup chopped parsley
¼ pound spinach, washed thoroughly and chopped
1 cup pomegranate juice
½ teaspoon oregano
2 teaspoons salt
¼ teaspoon pepper

Garnish
2 tablespoons chopped fresh mint
2 tablespoons chopped fresh coriander *
2 tablespoons pomegranate seeds

Sauté sliced onion in butter in heavy kettle until golden. Add lentils, cover with 8 cups of water, and bring to a boil. Cover kettle and cook over low heat for 30 minutes. Add rice, parsley, spinach, and pomegranate juice, and season with oregano, salt, and pepper. Simmer for 45 minutes and serve, garnished with fresh chopped mint and coriander and pomegranate seeds.
Serves 6.

* Available in Hispanic and Oriental groceries.

Chicken in Pomegranate Sauce

This is a traditional Persian dish, Fesenjan, with a deep, thick sauce, made also with duck or cubed lamb and served with rice.

INGREDIENTS
3 tablespoons butter
1 large onion, thinly sliced
1 three-pound chicken, cut into pieces
1 cup chicken broth
¾ cup walnuts, finely ground
3 tablespoons pomegranate syrup (see preceding recipe)
1 tablespoon sugar
½ teaspoon turmeric
¼ teaspoon cinnamon
¼ teaspoon black pepper
¼ cup lemon juice

Garnish
2 tablespoons finely chopped walnuts

Melt butter in heavy saucepan and sauté sliced onion until golden. Remove onion, add chicken pieces, and sauté until lightly browned. Return onions to pan, add broth, bring to a boil, and simmer covered for 30 minutes. Transfer chicken to dish and allow to cool. Combine ground walnuts, ½ cup water, pomegranate syrup, and sugar in pan and cook over low heat about 10 minutes or until sauce is smooth and hot. Bone chicken, cutting meat into small pieces, and return to pan. Add turmeric, cinnamon, pepper, and lemon juice, cover, and simmer for about an hour, when the sauce should be thick and dark. Add more lemon juice or sugar if necessary, according to taste. Transfer to serving dish and sprinkle with chopped walnuts. Serve with rice.
Serves 4.

Pomegranate Marinade

This marinade adds a fruity flavor to barbecued or broiled pork, lamb, or beef.

INGREDIENTS
1 cup pomegranate juice
1 onion, chopped
2 cloves garlic, minced
1 teaspoon oregano
½ teaspoon salt
¼ teaspoon pepper

Combine ingredients in a large bowl and mix well. Add cubed meat or chops to be barbecued or broiled and allow to marinate for at least several hours, mixing occasionally, before cooking.
Makes approximately 1¼ cups.

Pomegranate-Mint Chutney

INGREDIENTS
¼ cup pomegranate seeds
1 medium onion, chopped
1 green chili pepper, seeded and chopped
2 tablespoons chopped fresh mint
juice of half lemon
¼ teaspoon salt

Combine all ingredients in a blender and blend well to the consistency of a paste, but with a somewhat gritty texture. Serve as a condiment with curries or grilled meats.
Makes approximately ¾ cup.

Pomegranate Nut Dessert

In North Africa and the Middle East, pomegranate desserts are perfumed with the addition of a few drops of rose or orange flower-water. *

INGREDIENTS
seeds of 2 pomegranates
1 cup almonds, chopped
2 tablespoons sugar

Press pomegranate seeds with a spoon against the side of a bowl to liberate some of their juice. Add chopped almonds and sugar and mix well. Serve chilled.
Serves 4.

* Available in specialty shops or Middle Eastern groceries.

Pomegranate-Honey Jelly

INGREDIENTS
4 cups pomegranate juice
¼ cup lemon juice
5½ cups orange blossom or other mild honey
1 bottle (6 ounces) liquid pectin

Combine pomegranate and lemon juices in a deep kettle and heat. Stir in honey with a wooden spoon, mix well, and bring liquid to a boil over high heat. Stir in liquid pectin and continue cooking at a rolling boil for one minute, stirring constantly. Remove from heat and skim off foam with metal spoon. Ladle immediately into hot, sterilized jars, and seal immediately (see Appendix A, p. 138, for A Note on Preserving).
Makes 9 half-pint jars.

Quince

Golden apples: Greek myth delights in them, weaving their corruptive influence into tales of love and greed. The golden apple of discord, awarded by Paris to Aphrodite for the love of Helen, launched the Trojan War. Aphrodite, goddess of love herself, directed Hippomenes to distract swift Atalanta from her footrace by dropping golden fruits in her path. Apples were transmuted into gold by the touch of Midas, and Heracles voyaged to the end of the world to attain golden apples from the garden of the Hesperides. Scholars have sought to identify these wondrous fruits, suggesting, for example, that the apples of the Hesperides were actually the oranges and lemons that the Greeks had been told were flourishing in the distant land of Spain. But it could as well have been the common quince, which turned a brilliant "gilded" yellow as it ripened in the Mediterranean sun, that inspired ancient bards to sing of fruits of a still purer gold.

The Greeks brought quinces by ship from the island of Crete, or Cydonia, as they called it, and quinces were known to them simply as apples of Cydonia. As the cultivation of this fruit moved westward— quinces had originated in Persia and the Caucasus—the name of Cydonia was linked with it and was Latinized by the Romans. As the quince was slowly introduced into the rest of Europe over the succeeding centuries, this connection was retained in different European tongues, and it is still celebrated in the botanical name that the fruit bears today, *Cydonia oblonga*. Eventually the name became *coing* in French and *cuoyne* in Old English, its plural, *cuoynes*, giving us the name *quince* by which these golden fruits are called today.

HOW TO SELECT QUINCES

Until recently in America, quinces could only be obtained from trees on old farms or in neglected orchards, whose stock probably dated back to the plants brought here during colonial times, when quinces were a quite popular fruit. In the last few years, however, West Coast orchards have been cultivating quinces for distribution, and these are now becoming plentiful, not just in specialty shops but in supermarkets as well. Quinces are at their peak after the first frost, from late October through December, but they are found in markets well into February. When ripe, quinces are hard and pear-shaped, a deep lemon yellow in color, and very aromatic. On the tree, they are covered with a grayish fuzz, but this may be removed by the time the fruits are brought to market, and commercially grown quinces, curiously, also lack their distinctive aroma. Select fruits that are fully yellow, well formed, and free from blemishes, although if jams or jellies are to be made, imperfect quinces from neglected trees—or even those with worm holes—can readily be used after the bad parts are cut away. (It is said that quince trees thrive on neglect, and surely old quince trees are often heavily laden with ripening fruit, however imperfect their condition.) Quinces, like apples, may be stored in a cool place for several months.

HOW TO PREPARE QUINCES

Owing to their astringency, quinces are not generally eaten raw. Yet, writers over the centuries have mentioned types of quinces that were suitable for table use and Luther Burbank hoped that the variety he developed—the pineapple quince—would become popular for eating out of hand. Quinces are excellent for cooking, however, for they hold their shape well and do not become limp or mushy easily. They also add color to the plate: When they are well cooked, their pale flesh takes on a lovely salmon-pink hue. While quinces have fallen from popularity in this century, they have been documented in cookery since at least two thousand years ago, when the Roman epicure Apicius recorded recipes for stewing quinces (with leeks and honey) and for preserving them.

Quinces, like apples, are generally pared and cored before cooking. In eastern Europe, the Near East, and North Africa, they are often cooked with meat and poultry, stuffed like squashes with mixtures of meat, or included in stews. In northern Europe, quinces are more likely to appear in sweets; they may be baked whole like apples or included in puddings and in pies, alone or to enhance the flavor of apples. Beautiful deep red preserves, jellies, and jams are made from quinces, and the dark pastes made from cooking down quince purée with sugar are known throughout the Continent and Latin America.

About 3 pounds of quinces will make 6 cups when sliced and 1½ to 2 cups when boiled and puréed.

Persian Stuffed Quinces

INGREDIENTS
4 quinces, halved and cored
¼ cup yellow split peas
1 onion, coarsely chopped
4 tablespoons butter
½ pound lean ground lamb
1 tablespoon parsley, minced
¼ teaspoon cinnamon
½ teaspoon salt
⅛ teaspoon pepper

Garnish
sugar

Place halved quinces cut side up in baking dish and add about ½ inch water to dish. Cover loosely with foil and bake in a 350-degree oven about an hour, or until quinces are soft and easily pierced with a knife. Remove from oven and allow to cool. Meanwhile, put split peas in a saucepan in water to cover, bring to a boil, and simmer, covered, about a half-hour or until soft. In a frying pan, sauté onion in 2 tablespoons butter until golden, add ground lamb, and cook until meat is well browned. Remove pulp from cooked quinces, leaving a shell about ½-inch thick all around, and chop pulp. Add pulp to frying pan with drained split peas, parsley, cinnamon, salt, and pepper. Mix and sauté a few minutes longer to allow flavors to blend. Preheat oven to 350 degrees. Stuff quince halves with meat mixture, mounding each as necessary, and place in the baking dish. Dot tops with remaining butter and add ½ inch of water to dish. Bake covered for a half-hour to heat stuffed quinces thoroughly. Remove from oven, sprinkle with sugar, and serve.
Serves 4.

Stewed Beef with Quinces

INGREDIENTS
1 onion, coarsely chopped
2 tablespoons vegetable oil
1½ pounds stewing beef, cut into 1-inch cubes
½ teaspoon salt
⅛ teaspoon pepper
2 quinces, peeled, cored, and cut into 1-inch cubes
2 tablespoons butter
1 teaspoon sugar
¼ teaspoon cinnamon
juice of half lemon

In a heavy saucepan, sauté onion in oil over medium heat until golden. Add cubed beef and cook until brown on all sides. Season with salt and pepper and add 1 cup water. Reduce heat, cover, and cook slowly until meat is tender— about 45 minutes. Meanwhile, in a frying pan, stew quince cubes gently in butter, sugar, and cinnamon with 1 tablespoon water, covered, until tender—about 15 minutes. Add quinces to stew, sprinkle with lemon juice, and continue to cook uncovered for 15 minutes more.
Serves 4.

Quince Pudding

INGREDIENTS
4 quinces, peeled, cored, and coarsely chopped
½ cup heavy cream
¼ cup sugar
2 eggs, lightly beaten

Preheat oven to 375 degrees. In a kettle, cover quinces with water, bring to a boil, and simmer until fruit is soft. Drain and press fruit

through a sieve or food mill, to make about 1½ to 2 cups of quince purée. Combine quince purée with cream, sugar, and eggs, and mix well. Turn into a buttered 1-quart soufflé dish or baking dish and bake for 45 minutes or until pudding is well set.
Serves 4.

Quince Tart

INGREDIENTS
1 nine-inch sweet pie crust (see Appendix B, p. 140)

or

Gallete dough:
1 cup sifted flour
1 tablespoon sugar
½ teaspoon salt
5 tablespoons butter, softened
1 egg yolk
2 tablespoons milk

Filling:
4 tablespoons butter
3 cups peeled, cored, and thinly sliced quinces
4 tablespoons sugar
¼ cup heavy cream
1 egg, lightly beaten

Garnish
1 tablespoon sugar

Prepare a 9-inch sweet pie shell or make a tart shell out of galette dough: Sift together flour, sugar, and salt into a mixing bowl and cut in 5 tablespoons softened butter with pastry blender or two knives and work in well. Mix egg yolk and milk together and work into dough until ingredients are well combined. Form dough into a ball and chill.

Meanwhile, prepare filling: In an enamel frying pan, melt 4 tablespoons butter and add finely sliced quinces and 4 tablespoons sugar. Mix to coat well. Add 3 tablespoons water and cook gently, mixing occasionally, for about 20 minutes or until fruit is just soft and can be pierced with a fork. Allow to cool.

Preheat oven to 350 degrees. Meanwhile, press dough into 9-inch tart pan or pie plate and chill until fruit is ready. Arrange quince slices in circular pattern on pie crust. Spoon syrup that is left in frying pan over quinces, taking care not to let liquid overflow. Bake for about 30 minutes, until quinces begin to brown. In a bowl, beat egg and cream lightly, pour over tart, and bake about 10 minutes longer or until custard is just set. Remove from oven, sprinkle with 1 tablespoon sugar, and serve warm.

Makes 1 nine-inch pie.

Middle Eastern Quince-Marmalade Custard

INGREDIENTS
2½ cups milk
¼ cup sugar
4 tablespoons arrowroot or cornstarch
¼ cup quince marmalade (see preceding recipe)
1 teaspoon vanilla
3 teaspoons chopped, blanched almonds

Garnish
chopped almonds
cinnamon

Combine 2 cups milk with sugar in a saucepan, bring to a boil, and cook until sugar is dissolved. In a small bowl, combine cornstarch with ½ cup milk and mix well. Lower heat under saucepan and add cornstarch mixture, quince marmalade, vanilla, and chopped almonds, and continue to stir over low heat until custard thickens. Ladle into individual dessert dishes and garnish with chopped almonds and sprinkle with cinnamon. Chill well before serving.

Serves 4.

Quince Marmalade

The word marmalade, *originally designating a jam made from quinces, derives from* marmelo, *their Portuguese name.*

INGREDIENTS
3 cups quinces, peeled, cored, and coarsely grated
3 cups sugar
2 tablespoons lemon juice

In a kettle, cover quinces with water (about 3 cups), bring to a boil, and cook until they begin to soften—about 20 minutes. Add sugar and stir until it dissolves. Continue to cook over medium heat stirring occasionally, until quinces turn a deep pink color, about 45 minutes, and jam is at the setting stage. Add lemon juice, bring to a boil, ladle into hot, sterilized jars, and seal immediately (see Appendix A, p. 138, for A Note on Preserving).
Makes 4 half-pint jars.

Quince Paste

Quince paste or "cheese" is one of the oldest methods of preserving quinces, used wherever quinces are grown. As dulce de membrilo, *it is common throughout the Spanish world, served on bread or with cream cheese as a snack or dessert. As* cotignac, *a specialty of the French city of Orléans, orange juice and spices are added to the recipe.*

INGREDIENTS
4 pounds ripe quinces, peeled, cored, and coarsely chopped
2 cups sugar

In a deep kettle, cover quinces with water and boil gently until quinces are very soft, about a half-hour. Drain and pass quinces through a sieve or food mill. Measure 2 cups of quince purée, add equal amount of sugar to kettle, and stir well. Cook over medium heat, stirring constantly with a wooden spoon while mixture bubbles and cooks down to a deep red color. This may take as much as an hour or more. When quince paste is thick and will stay away from sides of kettle when stirred, remove from fire and spread into a baking dish to about ½-inch thick. Allow to sit for several days in an oven with a pilot light, or, more traditionally, in the sun (covered with cheesecloth), until it is firm and can be sliced. Cut into squares or decorative shapes with small cookie cutters and store between sheets of wax paper in a tightly covered container.

Paradise Jelly

Apples, cranberries, and quinces make a heavenly combination in taste and hue.

INGREDIENTS
2 pounds ripe quinces, peeled, cored, and coarsely chopped
2 pounds apples, peeled, cored, and coarsely chopped
2 cups cranberries
4 cups sugar

In a kettle, cover quinces with water, bring to a boil, and simmer until fruit is soft, about 30 minutes. Meanwhile, in a separate kettle, combine apples and cranberries, cover with water, bring to a boil, and simmer until fruit is soft, about 20 minutes. Put the softened fruits and liquid in a damp jelly bag or a colander lined with a double layer of dampened cheesecloth over a bowl and allow the juice to drip through. (Do not press or squeeze, or jelly will become cloudy.) In a deep kettle, combine 4 cups of the mixed juices with 4 cups of sugar and stir well until sugar is dissolved. Boil the liquid over a high flame until jelly mixture is at setting stage. Remove from heat and skim foam from top. Ladle immediately into hot, sterilized half-pint jars and seal (see Appendix A, p. 138, for A Note on Preserving).
Makes 4 half-pint jars.

Pickled Quinces

INGREDIENTS
2½ pounds ripe quinces, peeled, cored, and cut into ¼-inch slices
2 cups sugar
1¾ cups cider vinegar
1 teaspoon whole cloves
1 teaspoon whole allspice
2 four-inch pieces of cinnamon

Place quinces in a kettle, cover with water, bring to a boil, and simmer until quinces become just tender, about 20 minutes. Drain and reserve. In a deep kettle, combine sugar and vinegar and 1 cup water and bring to a boil, stirring until sugar dissolves. Tie spices in a cheesecloth bag and add to kettle. Simmer for 10 minutes; then add cooked quinces. Simmer gently until quinces begin to deepen in color, about 15 or 20 minutes longer. Remove spices and ladle quinces into hot, sterilized jars. Bring syrup back to boil, strain over quinces, and seal immediately (see Appendix A, p. 138, for A Note on Preserving).
Makes approximately 5 half-pint jars.

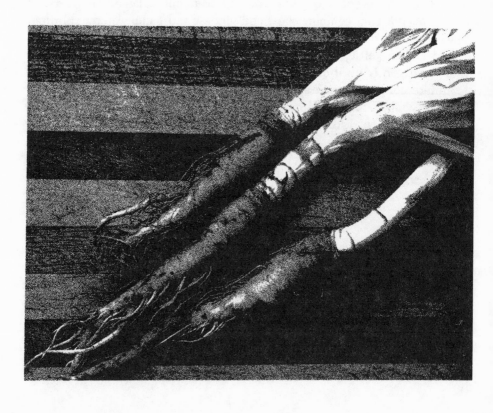

Salsify
(Oyster Plant)

Favored as a winter vegetable in France and Italy, salsify is not common in America today, although it was often included in the menus of our founding fathers. Thomas Jefferson listed it among his crops as early as 1774, and he grew it regularly in his garden at Monticello. In 1809, for example, he sowed "320 feet each salsafy & carrots which is very ample provision for my table"—and considerably more than he planted that year of our two more common root crops, beets and parsnips. Nineteenth-century American cookbooks regard salsify as a standard vegetable, and it must have been widely grown here at one time, for this foreign plant, brought from Europe for cultivation in kitchen gardens, has become naturalized. Better known as the wildflower *goatsbeard*, its purple flowers now dot meadows and roadsides along most of the East Coast.

Flower and food, this plant is called by several names. *Goatsbeard*, alluding to its silky white seed head not unlike that of a dandelion, is a direct translation of its botanical name, *Tragopogon porrifolius* ("goatsbeard with leeklike leaves"). The derivation and meaning of salsify have stumped etymologists, although related names appear in Spanish, Portuguese, Italian, French, and Persian. There is no doubt, however, as to the origin of the alternate names *oyster plant* and *vegetable oyster*, for the roots have a faint oysterlike flavor when cooked.

HOW TO SELECT SALSIFY

Salsify may be found in specialty grocery shops and at farm stands, and it has recently become popular with home gardeners. It first appears in markets in early fall, although, like so many other winter vegetables, its flavor is said to be improved by frost and it is better left in the ground longer. If it is mulched well, salsify may remain in the ground all winter (except in harshest regions) and dug for use as necessary. The tapering white roots, like parsnips in appearance though somewhat more slender, are best used when they are 7 to 9 inches long and 1 to 1½ inches in diameter. They should be firm, regular, and free of soft spots or blemishes. Salsify will remain crisp for a week or two if it is kept in a tightly closed plastic bag in the refrigerator. Scorzonera (*Scorzonera hispanica*), a root similar in shape but with black skin, is often sold as "black salsify."

HOW TO PREPARE SALSIFY

Salsify may be treated like other root vegetables, although its flavor is more subtle than that of carrots or parsnips, for example. Salsify is never eaten raw. It can be served very simply—baked, boiled, or puréed; or cold (boiled) with a vinaigrette dressing. It is used widely in Europe, especially in French and Italian cooking, where it is most often sautéed or fried (after parboiling) and served with a variety of typical sauces. Dishes that exploit its oystery taste are mostly English or American in origin.

Salsify discolors rapidly on being scraped or cut; thus it should be dropped into acidulated water (water with vinegar added, 1 teaspoon to each quart) immediately after scraping. In recipes calling for parboiled salsify, the roots need not be scraped first; instead, they should be scrubbed well with a vegetable brush, trimmed top and bottom, dropped into salted boiling water, and cooked for about 30 to 45 minutes, depending on thickness of roots and tenderness desired. When it is cooked this way and refreshed under cold water, the skin can be easily peeled away with the fingers. One pound of salsify will make about one cup of purée. Scorzonera may be treated like salsify but should always be scraped before using. Canned salsify, imported from Europe and found on shelves of "gourmet" shops, is suitable for most recipes calling for parboiled roots.

Mock Oyster Soup

INGREDIENTS
1 onion, minced
2 tablespoons butter
1 pound salsify, trimmed, scraped, and cut into ¼-inch cubes
1 small potato, diced
1 stalk celery, diced
4 cups milk
1 teaspoon salt
¼ teaspoon white pepper

Garnish
butter
paprika
oyster crackers

Sauté minced onion in butter in a heavy kettle over medium flame until translucent. Add diced salsify, potato, celery, milk, salt, and pepper, and bring almost to a boil. Lower heat, cover, and simmer about 30 minutes or until vegetables are tender. Remove vegetables from liquid with slotted spoon and purée all but ½ cup in blender, or put through a sieve. Return purée to kettle and mix well with liquid. Add reserved vegetables and reheat, but do not boil. Serve garnished with butter, paprika, and oyster crackers.
Serves 4.

Chicken Pie with Salsify and Carrots

INGREDIENTS
1 3½ pound chicken, cut into pieces
3 cups boiling water
1 teaspoon salt
1 ten-inch savory pie shell and crust (see Appendix B, p. 140)
1 egg white
3 salsify roots, trimmed, scraped, quartered lengthwise,
  and cut into ½-inch lengths
2 carrots, quartered lengthwise and cut into 1½-inch lengths
2 tablespoons butter
2 tablespoons flour
1 teaspoon celery seed
1 tablespoon parsley, chopped
pinch cayenne

Put chicken pieces into a large kettle and add 3 cups boiling water and salt. Return to a boil over medium flame, reduce heat, cover, and simmer until chicken is tender, about 1 to 1½ hours. Meanwhile, prepare double recipe for pie crust, and line a 10-inch pie plate with pastry, reserving half of dough for top. Brush with egg white. When chicken is cooked, remove to a plate to cool. Bring broth back to a boil and add salsify and carrots; reduce heat, cover, and simmer for about 20 minutes or until vegetables are tender. Remove from broth with slotted spoon. Remove chicken from bones, cut meat into pieces, and combine with cooked vegetables. Fill pie shell with mixture of chicken, salsify, and carrots.

Preheat oven to 450 degrees. Strain enough broth to make 1½ cups. In a saucepan, melt butter over low heat and add flour; blend in well with wire whisk, mixing constantly for several minutes. Add the strained broth and stir well. Cook until sauce comes to a boil and is smooth and begins to thicken. Stir in celery seed and chopped parsley, and add cayenne. Pour immediately over chicken and vegetables in pie shell. Cover with pie crust and press edges down all around. Prick top with fork in several places and bake for a half-hour until crust is well browned.
Serves 6.

Salsify Fritters

INGREDIENTS
1 pound salsify, well scrubbed
¼ cup olive oil
2 tablespoons lemon juice
2 tablespoons chopped parsley
¼ teaspoon salt
⅛ teaspoon pepper
½ cup flour
1 teaspoon baking powder
¼ teaspoon salt
2 eggs, lightly beaten
½ cup milk
oil for deep frying

Cook salsify in salted boiling water until barely tender, about a half-hour. Refresh in cold water and skin. Cut salsify lengthwise into quarters and then into 3-inch lengths. In a bowl combine oil, lemon juice, chopped parsley, salt, and pepper, and marinate parboiled salsify in it for about a half-hour, mixing occasionally to make sure salsify is well coated. Meanwhile, make a batter in a separate bowl by combining flour, baking powder, and salt, and adding beaten eggs and milk. Mix until batter is smooth. Let batter sit for at least a half-hour. Drain salsify, dip in batter to coat well, and fry in batches in hot oil until golden brown.
Serves 4.

Mock Oysters

INGREDIENTS
4 salsify roots, well scrubbed
1 egg
1 cup fine breadcrumbs
½ teaspoon salt
oil for frying

Garnish
tartar sauce
lemon wedges

Drop salsify into salted boiling water and cook until barely tender—about a half-hour. Drain, refresh under cold water, and skin. Slice salsify roots diagonally into rounds about ¾-inch thick. Beat egg in a bowl with two tablespoons water until frothy. Dip salsify pieces into egg and then into breadcrumbs seasoned with ½ teaspoon salt, then into the egg and breadcrumbs again, making sure they are well coated. Allow to sit for about a half-hour and then fry in 1 inch of hot oil until golden on both sides. Serve with tartar sauce, garnished with lemon wedges.
Serves 4.

Salsify Provençale

INGREDIENTS
1 pound salsify, well scrubbed
2 tablespoons oil
2 tablespoons butter
1 clove garlic, finely minced
1 tablespoon chopped parsley

SALSIFY

Cook salsify in salted boiling water until tender, about 30 minutes. Refresh under cold running water, drain, and skin. Cut salsify in half lengthwise and across into 3-inch lengths. Heat oil and butter in a frying pan over medium flame. Add parboiled salsify and sauté until golden on both sides. Add minced garlic and parsley, mix well, and sauté several minutes more.
Serves 4.

Salsify with Stewed Vegetables

INGREDIENTS
1 pound salsify, well scrubbed
1 onion, chopped
2 tablespoons butter
1 carrot, diced
1 small turnip, diced
1 stalk celery, diced
¼ teaspoon salt
1 tablespoon chopped parsley
⅛ teaspoon pepper
⅛ teaspoon nutmeg
3 tablespoons milk
1 tablespoon lemon juice

Cook salsify in salted boiling water until it is tender, about 30 minutes. Drain, refresh in cold water, skin, and cut into 3-inch lengths. Meanwhile, in a large saucepan, sauté onion in butter over medium flame until golden. Add diced carrot, turnip, celery, and salt, mix well, and sauté 2 minutes. Add 1 tablespoon water, cover, and stew over medium flame for 20 minutes or until vegetables are tender. Add cooked salsify and mix well. Season with parsley, pepper, and nutmeg, add milk, sprinkle with lemon juice, and stir. Cover and cook 5 minutes longer.
Serves 4.

Salsify Batter Cakes

INGREDIENTS
1 egg, lightly beaten
½ cup milk
½ cup flour
½ teaspoon salt
1 teaspoon baking powder
1 pound salsify, trimmed, scraped, and grated
oil for frying

Beat egg and milk together in a bowl. Combine flour, salt, and baking powder and add to milk and egg, mixing well to make a good batter. Add grated salsify, mix, and drop by spoonfuls into 1 inch of hot oil. Fry until cakes are golden on both sides.
Serves 4.

Scalloped Salsify

INGREDIENTS
2 cups warm, puréed, parboiled salsify
¼ cup milk
2 tablespoons softened butter
½ teaspoon salt
1 tablespoon chopped parsley
pinch cayenne
1 egg, lightly beaten
3 tablespoons breadcrumbs
2 tablespoons melted butter

Preheat oven to 375 degrees. Combine puréed salsify, milk, butter, and salt, and beat until smooth. Add chopped parsley, cayenne, and beaten egg, and stir in well. Turn into a buttered 6-inch soufflé or round baking dish. Sprinkle breadcrumbs on top, drizzle with melted butter, and bake until top is brown and the purée well heated—about 20 minutes.
Serves 4.

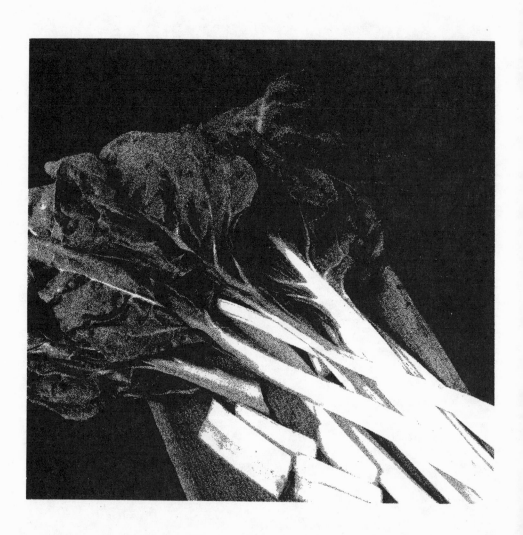

Swiss Chard

Swiss chard combines two vegetables in one: Its large green or red leaves and its broad, celerylike stalks are usually prepared separately and have distinct culinary traditions. Swiss chard is especially popular in France, where, depending on the region, the leaf (called *blette* or *bette*) or the stalk (called *carde*) is preferred, with classic French cooking favoring the latter. Chard apparently owes its name to French confusion between chard stalks and the larger but somewhat similar cardoon, a vegetable adored by the French. Both are sometimes called *carde* in French, and this name came into English as chard. The connection with Switzerland is more obscure, for chard does not grow there in great abundance. One might conjecture that shipments of chard from that direction were once dubbed "Swiss" *carde* (chard) to distinguish them from what was considered the more common variety, or "French" *carde* (cardoons).

The name *chard* obscures the close relationship that this vegetable has with the familiar beet; while chard does not form a fleshy root, a comparison of leaves makes their close ties obvious. Its alternative names, leafy or silver beet, and its botanical name (*Beta vulgaris cicla*, or "common beet") confirm the connection. Leafy beets, mentioned as early as the fourth century B.C. by Aristotle, are native to the Mediterranean region and the Near East and were probably among the first green vegetables to be cultivated. They were widely used as one of the greens added to the soup pot by peasants throughout Europe; in 1629, the Englishman John Parkinson considered them very ordinary in his famous *Paradisus in Sole*, noting that "Beetes, both white, greene and red, are put into the pot among other herbes, to make pottage, as is commonly known unto all." Their cousin, the red beet, was of more interest to him, however, having been grown in England for only a few decades at that time.

HOW TO SELECT SWISS CHARD

Swiss chard, a plant that withstands hot weather well, is in season when spinach and other delicate greens may be less common—from early summer throughout the fall. It also appears sporadically in specialty markets throughout the year, especially in early spring. Chard is brought to market tied in bunches of separate leaves and stalks; both light and dark green and reddish varieties are sold, the stalks being white or red. Like other greens, the leaves should be of an even color, without blemishes and not wilted; the stalks, like celery, should be crisp and should snap readily when bent. Young, tender leaves are about 5 to 8 inches in length. Older ones will grow considerably longer; while they tend to be tougher and take longer to cook, they are quite suitable for cooking. Washed and trimmed leaves may be stored in a plastic bag in the refrigerator for several days; stalks will keep there much longer in an airtight plastic bag. Swiss chard is particularly well suited for freezing: Remove ribs and stalks and plunge leaves in boiling water for 2 minutes; refresh in cold water, drain well, and store in closed containers in the freezer. The stalks may also be frozen: Washed and trimmed, they are boiled for 3 minutes, cooled in cold water, drained, and packed into containers for freezing.

HOW TO PREPARE SWISS CHARD

Swiss-chard leaves may be prepared like spinach or other greens (see Greens and Kale, chapters 5 and 7), and the stalks according to any recipe for cooking celery or asparagus. Chard leaves are often boiled quickly and served hot or cold with a dressing of oil and lemon juice or vinegar. They are used throughout the Mediterranean region in soups, stuffed like cabbage, and made into fillings for savory pastries and pastas. The stalks, parboiled or sautéed, are especially prized in France, where they are served hot or cold with any number of traditional sauces—cream, butter, cheese, aioli (the garlic mayonnaise of Provence), and *bagna cauda* (p. 24).

The somewhat bitter leaves of Swiss chard are not generally eaten raw, but when they are young and very tender, they will add interest to salads. The stalks and leaves should be washed thoroughly, although chard is not generally as dirty as spinach. After removing the stalks, the ribs should be cut out from the leaves, which is best done with a scissor or by folding the leaf in half and slicing along the stalk.

The leaves are generally coarsely shredded or chopped and then boiled, or steamed in the water that clings to them, until tender, about 10 to 20 minutes. The stalks should be treated like celery: trimmed well and strings removed. One pound of chard leaves will make about 6 cups of coarsely chopped leaves and 2 to 3 cups boiled or wilted greens.

Swiss Chard Appetizer

This is a spicy dish eaten as an hors d'oeuvre in Israel by Sephardic immigrants from North Africa.

INGREDIENTS
3 pounds Swiss chard, leaves only, well washed and coarsely chopped
1 large onion, chopped
1 clove garlic, minced
½ teaspoon dried red pepper flakes
6 tablespoons olive oil
¼ teaspoon salt
juice of half lemon

Combine chard, onion, garlic, pepper flakes, and olive oil in a large, deep saucepan and cook, covered, over medium heat for about 20 minutes, mixing occasionally, until leaves are reduced. Lower heat and cook slowly, covered, for about an hour longer, stirring occasionally, until chard becomes a thick, deep green mass. Transfer to a serving dish, sprinkle with salt and lemon juice, and allow to cool. Serve at room temperature.
Serves 6.

Swiss Chard Pastries (Boreks)

These crispy Turkish pastries are served as appetizers.

INGREDIENTS
2 pounds Swiss chard, leaves only, well washed and coarsely chopped
1 large onion, coarsely chopped
2 tablespoons butter
1 egg, lightly beaten
¼ teaspoon allspice
¼ teaspoon cinnamon
¼ teaspoon salt
6 sheets phylo pastry (12 × 17 inch), about ¼ pound *
4 tablespoons melted butter

Steam chard in the water that clings to the leaves after washing, covered, until tender, about 10 minutes, mixing once or twice, and drain well. Meanwhile, sauté onion in 2 tablespoons butter in a frying pan until golden. In a bowl, combine drained chard, onion, and lightly beaten egg; add allspice, cinnamon, and salt, and mix well.

Preheat oven to 350 degrees. Prepare the phylo pastry for stuffing, keeping in mind that it dries out very quickly and should be covered with a damp cloth when not being worked on. First place the 6 sheets of pastry on top of each other and roll up into a cylinder. Cut crosswise into 4 sections, each about 3 inches wide. Put 3 sections aside covered, and unroll fourth section carefully. One by one, spread strips on board or waxed paper and brush with melted butter. Place a teaspoon of filling near bottom of the strip and fold bottom edge up and across the filling to make an open triangle. Fold this triangle over again, alternating back and forth from side to side until the entire strip is used and the pastry is completed. Place on cookie sheet and continue to fill and fold strips until all are used up. Butter tops of triangles and bake until brown, about a half-hour.
Makes 24 miniature pastries.

* Phylo pastry is available in 1-pound packages in Middle Eastern grocery shops.

Cream of Swiss Chard Soup

INGREDIENTS
1 onion, chopped
3 tablespoons butter
1 pound Swiss chard, leaves only, well washed and coarsely chopped
2 cups chicken broth
1 cup milk
1 teaspoon salt
¼ teaspoon freshly ground pepper

Garnish
4 tablespoons sour cream
2 scallions, chopped
paprika

Sauté onion in butter in a large saucepan over medium heat until translucent. Add chard, cover, reduce heat, and cook for 10 minutes or until chard is completely wilted and tender. Purée in blender until mixture is of a smooth consistency. Return to saucepan and add broth, milk, salt, and pepper, stirring until well mixed. Heat soup well but do not boil. Serve hot or well chilled, garnishing each portion with a tablespoon of sour cream, chopped scallion, and paprika.
Serves 4.

Lebanese Stuffed Swiss Chard Leaves (Dolmas)

INGREDIENTS

24 young Swiss chard leaves, well washed and stalks removed
1 onion, finely chopped
1 clove garlic, minced
2 tablespoons olive oil
½ cup minced flat parsley
2 cups steamed rice
1 cup cooked or canned chick peas, well drained
2 tablespoons minced fresh mint
1 teaspoon salt
¼ teaspoon pepper
1 cup chicken broth
3 tablespoons lemon juice
½ teaspoon salt

Drop chard leaves individually into boiling water and blanch for a few seconds only. Remove and drop into cold water. Drain leaves well and reserve. In a small frying pan, sauté onion and garlic in olive oil until onion is translucent. Add minced parsley, mix, and sauté one minute more. In a bowl, combine steamed rice, chick peas, mint, salt, pepper, and onion-parsley mixture, and mix well. Place a chard leaf on a flat surface and put a tablespoon of stuffing mixture near one end. Roll leaves diagonally, folding sides in as leaf is rolled. Continue filling and rolling leaves until ingredients are used up. Arrange chard rolls tightly together in layers in a heavy 2-quart saucepan. Add broth, lemon juice, and salt, bring to a boil, cover, and cook over low heat for 30 minutes, taking care that rolls do not burn.
Makes 24 dolmas.

Cod and Swiss Chard Casserole

INGREDIENTS
1 pound salt cod, soaked for several hours
6 tablespoons olive oil
2 pounds Swiss chard, leaves only, well washed and coarsely chopped
2 cloves garlic, minced
¼ teaspoon salt
¼ teaspoon pepper
pinch nutmeg
2 tablespoons breadcrumbs

Boil soaked cod in water until it can easily be flaked, about 20 to 30 minutes. Drain and flake. Meanwhile, heat 4 tablespoons oil in a heavy frying pan. When it is hot, add the chard leaves, garlic, salt, pepper, and nutmeg. Toss well and cook, stirring occasionally, for 10 minutes.

Preheat oven to 350 degrees. Mix the cod with the chard and transfer to a baking dish. Sprinkle with breadcrumbs and remaining 2 tablespoons of oil, and brown gently in oven—about 20 to 30 minutes. *Serves 6.*

Buttered Swiss Chard

INGREDIENTS
2 pounds Swiss chard, well washed, leaves coarsely shredded, stalks
    trimmed and cut into 1-inch lengths
2 tablespoons butter
¼ teaspoon salt
juice of half lemon

Sauté chard stalks in butter in a large kettle for 2 minutes, stirring to coat them well. Add chard leaves with the water that clings after washing, and salt, and cook, covered, until leaves and stalks are tender—about 15 minutes. Uncover and cook several minutes longer so that any water in pot evaporates. Sprinkle with lemon juice and serve. *Serves 4.*

Swiss Chard Pie

Swiss chard pie, tourta de bléa, *is a specialty of Provence that is commonly sold in the markets of Nice.*

INGREDIENTS
1 nine-inch savory pie shell (see Appendix B, p. 140)
1½ pounds Swiss chard, leaves only, well washed and finely shredded
¼ pound gouda or mild cheddar cheese, grated
½ teaspoon salt
¼ teaspoon pepper
1 teaspoon sugar
2 tablespoons currants
2 tablespoons pine nuts
1 egg, lightly beaten

Garnish
1 teaspoon sugar

Prepare pie shell. Steam chard in the water that clings to the leaves after washing, covered, until well reduced, about 10 minutes, and drain well. Preheat oven to 375 degrees. In a bowl combine chard, cheese, salt, pepper, 1 teaspoon sugar, currants, and pine nuts, and mix well. Add egg to bind mixture and fill pie shell. Bake for 30 minutes or until crust is brown and filling is dry and bubbling. Remove from oven and sprinkle with 1 teaspoon sugar before serving.
Serves 6.

Salad of Swiss Chard Stalks, Roast Beef, and Capers

INGREDIENTS
Stalks of 2 pounds of Swiss chard, well washed and cut into 1-inch
  lengths
¼ pound cooked roast beef, cut into julienne strips
2 scallions, sliced
1 tablespoon capers
2 tablespoons salad oil
1 tablespoon vinegar
¼ teaspoon salt
freshly ground pepper (to taste)

Blanch chard stalks in boiling water for 2 minutes and refresh under cold
water. Drain well and arrange in salad bowl with roast beef, scallions,
and capers. Dress with oil and vinegar, season with salt, and pepper to
taste, and mix gently.
Serves 4.

Swiss Chard Stalks Parmesan

INGREDIENTS
Stalks of 3 pounds of Swiss chard, well washed and cut into 2-inch
  lengths
3 tablespoons butter
½ teaspoon salt
⅛ teaspoon pepper
¼ teaspoon nutmeg
3 tablespoons grated Parmesan cheese

Boil chard stalks for 5 minutes, until just tender, and drain well. In an
oven-proof frying pan, sauté chard stalks gently in butter until well
coated and limp. Season with salt, pepper, and nutmeg, and sprinkle
with grated cheese. Pass under the broiler until cheese melts and begins
to brown.
Serves 4.

Appendix A

Appendix A: A Note on Preserving

Home preserving is not as difficult as many people who have never done it suppose, but one should become familiar with the general procedures before starting. Instructions are given in standard cookbooks, such as *The Joy of Cooking*; in the many specialized cookbooks on canning and preserving now available; and in the series of United States Department of Agriculture *Home and Garden Bulletins*, which may be purchased at nominal cost from the Government Printing Office.

The basic equipment required for preserving includes a deep 8- to 10-quart kettle, a funnel or strainer, a ladle, and, for jellies, a jelly bag, or cheesecloth. In addition, suitable jelly glasses or preserving jars are required. The jars that are simplest to use are those with separate metal lids and bands, which can be easily and tightly sealed.

Jars should be well washed, sterilized in boiling water for 10 minutes, and then kept hot in the water or a slow oven until used, to prevent the jars from cracking when hot liquids are added. Fill the hot jars immediately when the mixture is ready; wipe the rims clean with a hot, damp cloth; place lids on the jars; and screw the metal rims down tightly. Allow jars to cool and store in a cool, dark place.

JELLIES, MARMALADES, AND BUTTERS

Fruit jellies, marmalades, and butters are prepared with pectin— either naturally occurring or added; acid, usually lemon juice; and sugar (or honey). The recipes in this book should give good results if the instructions are followed carefully, but since the amount of pectin in fruit varies, the time necessary for jellies and other preserves made without added pectin to reach the setting stage cannot be timed exactly.

The simplest method to test for the setting stage is to put a drop of boiling fruit mixture on a cold plate and put it in the freezer for several minutes. If it gels, the mixture should be done.

PICKLES, RELISHES, AND CHUTNEYS

The United States Government Department of Agriculture recommends that pickles, relishes, and chutneys be processed, that is, the filled, sealed jars be immersed in actively boiling water for a length of time (perhaps 5 or 10 minutes) depending on the food being processed. General instructions and times for processing can be found in the sources cited above. Traditionally, however, pickles, relishes, and chutneys have not been processed, and most basic cookbooks do not give such instructions for these recipes. Since the quantities given for the recipes in this book are small, one might take the precaution of storing the few jars of pickles or relishes in the refrigerator, which should keep them safe in any case. As with any preserved product, always check foods carefully before serving for signs of spoilage: leakage from jars, bulging lids, gases, mold, unpleasant odors, or mushy or slimy vegetables. *If there is even any suspicion of spoilage, do not eat—or even taste—the contents of the jar.*

Appendix B

Appendix B: Pie Crusts

QUICK SAVORY PIE CRUST

INGREDIENTS

1 cup plus 1 tablespoon sifted all-purpose flour
¾ teaspoon salt
¼ cup vegetable oil
2 tablespoons iced water

Sift together flour and salt. Pour oil and water together over flour and mix with a fork. Form dough into a ball and roll out on a lightly floured board or between two sheets of waxed paper. Line a 9- or 10-inch pie plate with dough, fill, and bake according to recipe. Double recipe for a two-crust pie, using slightly more than half the dough for bottom crust.

SWEET PIE CRUST

INGREDIENTS

¾ cup plus 2 tablespoons sifted all-purpose flour
2 tablespoons sugar
pinch salt
⅓ cup butter
2 teaspoons iced water

Sift together flour, sugar, and salt. With a pastry blender or two knives, cut in butter until flour has the consistency of rough cornmeal. Sprinkle with iced water to bind pastry and form into a ball. Roll out on a lightly floured board or between two sheets of waxed paper and line a 9-inch pie plate. Fill and bake according to recipe. For a baked pie shell, prick dough in several places with a fork and bake in a preheated 450-degree oven until brown, about 12 to 15 minutes. For a two-crust pie, double recipe, using slightly more than half the dough for bottom crust.

Index

Listings of recipes under general categories (*i.e.: appetizers, soups, etc.*) appear at the beginning of the book.

INDEX